CW01020776

WILFRID HERBERT GORE EWART

From a Painting by
Miss Nora Cundell

SCOTS GUARD

TO

SCOTS GUARDS,

PAST AND PRESENT,

AND TO THE MEMORY OF

FOUR BROTHER OFFICERS:

LIEUT. SIR EDWARD HULSE

LIEUT. HON. G. W. E. ELLIOT

LIEUT. A. R. W. MENZIES

SECOND LIEUT. L. A. JARVIS

SCOTS GUARD

On the Western Front, 1915-1918

Wilfrid Ewart

STRONG OAK PRESS

Publishing history: This work was first published in 1934, more than a decade after Ewart's untimely death in Mexico. This edition reproduces, unabridged, the major part of the work which deals with Ewart's record of the Great War and immediately afterwards. Omitted is that section of the work which covered the period after 1919.
This paperback edition published 2001.

ISBN: 1-871048-27-3

Published by THE STRONG OAK PRESS
PO BOX 47
STEVENAGE, HERTS, SG2 8UH, UK

Printed in Great Britain by Watkiss Studios, Biggleswade, Beds, UK

PROLOGUE

Wilfrid Herbert Gore Ewart was born on May 19, 1892. He was descended on both sides from a race of distinguished soldiers.

His father, Herbert Brisbane Ewart, is a son of the late Lieutenant-General Charles Brisbane Ewart, R.E., a Crimean veteran, afterwards Governor of Jersey and grandson of Lieutenant-General J. F. Ewart, C.B., whose younger son, General Sir John Ewart, G.C.B., 93rd Highlanders, was father of Lieutenant-General Sir Spencer Ewart, K.C.B., Cameron Highlanders, G.O.C. Scottish Command during the Great War.

His mother, Lady Mary Ewart, was the youngest daughter of the fourth Earl of Arran, K.P., and grand-daughter of General Sir William Napier, the historian of the Peninsular War, by his marriage with a daughter of his cousin, General Henry Fox, youngest brother of Charles James Fox. Sir William Napier was a younger brother of the general famous in India, Sir Charles Napier, and of General Sir George Napier; their mother and the mother of Charles and Henry Fox being daughters of the second Duke of Richmond.

Wilfrid Ewart's boyhood was marred by delicate health, which prevented his entering a public school, and on leaving his preparatory school, St. Aubyns, Rottingdean, he was sent to a private tutor at Parkstone. At this time he spent long and somewhat unconventional holidays with his father in Tyrol, where he would lie for hours in the mountains surrounded by wild birds, which he used to attract by some mysterious magnetism. Ewart's affection for birds extended also to the farmyard, and at the age of sixteen a work of his written in collaboration with J. Stephen Hicks, *The Possibilities of Modern Poultry Farming*, was published, having first been serialised in *Farm Life*. Three years later, in 1911, Ewart and Hicks followed this with another booklet, *Practical Poultry-keeping for Small-holders*. With these works to his credit and numerous articles on poultry being published in the press, Ewart between the ages of sixteen and nineteen often made as much as £100 a year by his pen.

In the summer of 1914 he was offered a post as secretary to Princess Dolgoruki at her house in Berkshire. But the War breaking out, he could not accept the appointment. Although bad health and eyesight quite unfitted him, he joined up; Lord Ruthven, his cousin, then a Major in the Scots Guards, suggesting his joining that regiment. A handsome, tall young man, Ewart was destined to be an officer popular with his men. However, the front was not to see him immediately on his becoming a soldier, for, in the few days' holiday granted him to clear up all his personal affairs, he met with a bicycle accident which delayed him six weeks. He then endured training at Caterham, went to Wellington Barracks, and was detailed for guard at Buckingham Palace. He was warned for draft, warned again, and yet did not go. He spent Christmas 1914 at home, saw the old year out, was warned again, and finally in mid-February 1915 (it is believed on Monday, February 15th), in charge of a draft, he left London.

It is at this point that his narrative commences.

CONTENTS

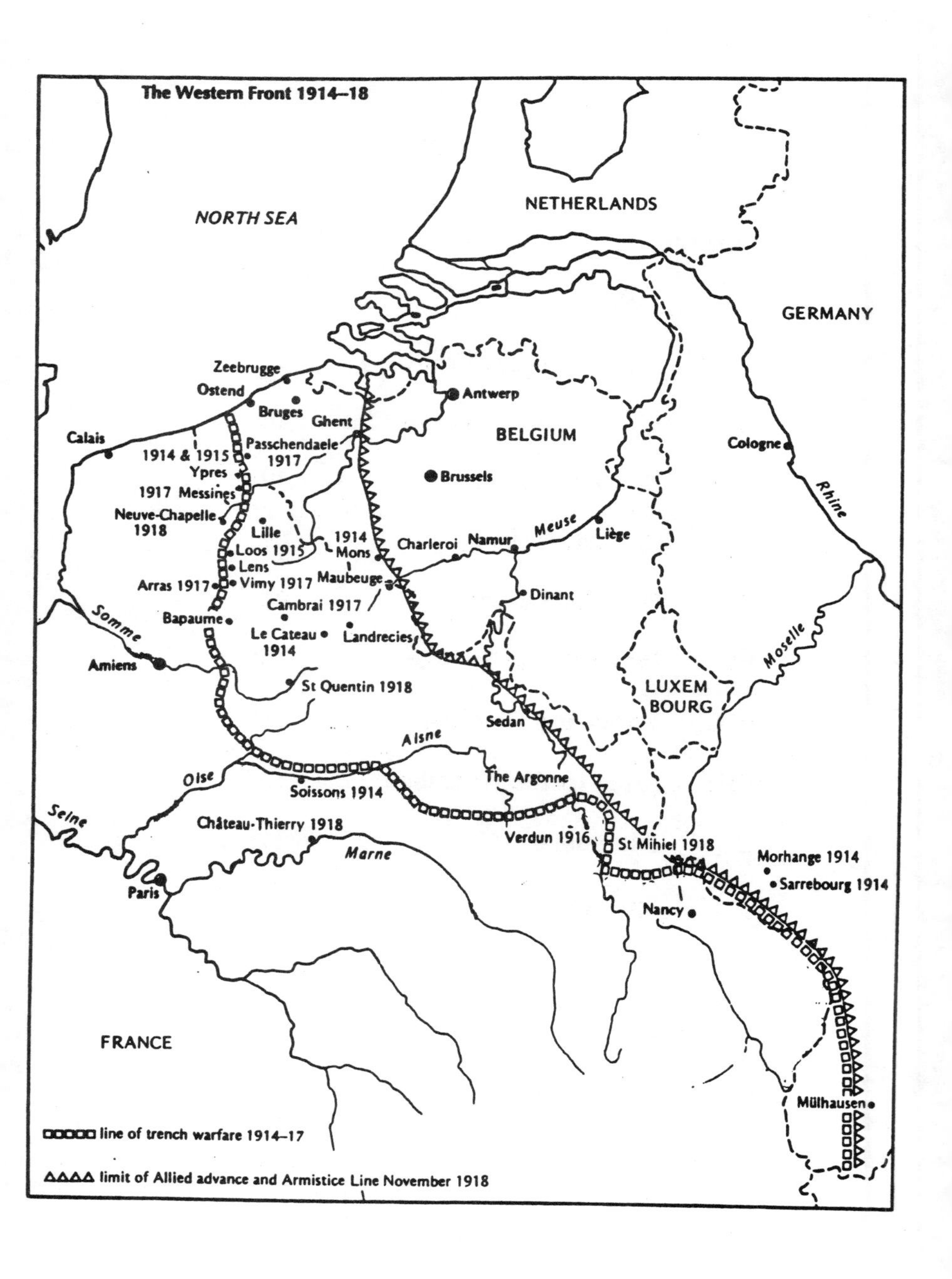
The Western Front 1914–18
NORTH SEA
NETHERLANDS
GERMANY
BELGIUM
LUXEM BOURG
FRANCE
Zeebrugge
Ostend
Bruges
Ghent
Antwerp
Calais
1914 & 1915
Passchendaele 1917
Ypres
1917 Messines
Neuve-Chapelle 1918
Lille
Loos 1915
Lens
Arras 1917
Vimy 1917
1914 Mons
Charleroi
Namur
Meuse
Liège
Brussels
Cologne
Rhine
Maubeuge
Cambrai 1917
Dinant
Bapaume
Le Cateau 1914
Landrecies
Somme
Amiens
St Quentin 1918
Moselle
Sedan
Aisne
Oise
Soissons 1914
The Argonne
Seine
Château-Thierry 1918
Marne
Verdun 1916
St Mihiel 1918
Morhange 1914
Sarrebourg 1914
Paris
Nancy
Mülhausen
line of trench warfare 1914–17
limit of Allied advance and Armistice Line November 1918

CHAPTER I

LONDON TO THE FRONT

We left London for Havre one brilliant sunny morning in mid-winter. It was ten o'clock. The blue mists had scarce lifted from the river, and the station was nearly empty save for the friends and relations of the two hundred and twelve men of my draft. Handkerchiefs were waved and the train steamed out just as a hundred other trains steam out week by week. We rattled through the smiling English countryside, through the commons and dark green pinewoods, through the open uplands and snug valleys, past a score of well-known, well-loved places.

Southampton was reached about two o'clock. The business of detraining and embarking took but a short time, for there was practically no baggage. But there were formalities and already other troops—one draft—aboard the little paddle-boat, which in normal times was a pleasure-boat on the Clyde. All afternoon we waited for the third and last draft to arrive. It came on board about four o'clock. And at about five-thirty in the early hours of a grey evening we glided down the harbour. The sun had long since disappeared and a nasty wind had begun to play with the sea. Past the bell-buoy, which rocked and tolled amid the rising waves, bidding farewell to every outward-going ship, we went, and so left the shore lights behind. The forts and lightship disappeared. The dim, swift-moving outline of a destroyer took their place against the darkening sea. There was a more than perceptible swell and the ship rolled dismally. Soon it became almost an obligation to feel sick. And presently five melancholy officers sat around their cabin—a veritable biscuit-box of a cabin—awaiting the end! To crown all, I was in supreme command, the senior officer on the boat! I was given a code-word, and in the midst of this nightmare had to decipher messages.

What a night! What sheets of rain! What a violent wind! It was a relief at last, after sleepless hours packed like sardines, with no cabins for the troops, to ride at anchor in port again. It was the middle of the night and had been a rough trip. We thought it would never end. A hulk of a French steamer, very low in the water, was towed slowly in through the driving rain and drifting sea-sand as we waited. She had been torpedoed two nights before. By degrees, and as, with anchor up again, we edged in towards the quay-side of Havre the men recovered their spirits—the poor wretches who had spent the night on deck, on the stairs, in the gangways down below, everywhere *in extremis!*

We landed after a considerable delay at about half-past ten of a rainy, windy morning, and had a five-mile march through the crowded streets to the camp at Honfleur on the hills behind the town. Past crowded wharves and yards and docks, great mountains of stores and lines of the A.S.C. wagons; past French Territorials, who presented arms; past smoky hideous factories, whence the workpeople were thronging to their midday meal. So through divers difficult streets to the straight French *pavé* road lined with poplars, which led by way of various suburbs to the base camp.

Such a brand-new town of canvas huts and white tents clinging to the hillside! None would believe that so vast an accumulation of dwellings could spring up in so short a time. The officers, it appeared, slept in canvas huts. I was drafted to one with a fellow subaltern, Jarvis, a very nice fellow, and we found it comfortable enough with our warm sleeping-bags and a canvas bucket that did duty for a bath between the two of us. The men were put in tents. The camp was bleak, but otherwise bearable. But the officers' mess was less so; it was a rare draughty place, with a tin roof and a long table on trestles, and we had to scramble at the board, nay, beg and pray for food. But there was no time to worry about anything, for the next day there was an inspection by the O.C. and the Medical Officer and various other parades. Ammunition had to be issued and deficiencies of kit made good. We were very busy and had not a moment to spare. Afterwards we worked all day at censoring hundreds of the men's letters, of which there seemed to be no end.

The second night there was a concert in the big tin Y.M.C.A. hut. The concert-party consisted of Lena Ashwell and four other well-known "stars," whom a few weeks before I had seen behind the brilliant footlights of the London stage. In Honfleur they were less brilliant to look upon, being in gum-boots and rough country clothes, muddy and somewhat dishevelled. They sang popular and old-fashioned sentimental airs, "The Chocolate Soldier" and "The Little Grey Home in the West," which brought down a "house" crammed from end to end with khaki. Afterwards they dined in our mess.

For five days we led a life of censoring, inspecting, and being inspected. Then—it was Saturday—the order came to be off. We were bound for the Front, which was a two days' journey, mainly in cattle-trucks, as I learned, so that it was not much to look forward to. However, neither was it much fun stopping at Honfleur. In Havre I had got the last few things I wanted and was at last fully equipped for the fray. It was time to be moving.

It was a sunny winter's afternoon, this Saturday of February 20th, 1915, and at about half-past three—I having made my requisite short address—we all marched with other drafts to the number of three thousand men four miles along the pretty valley road which led to the wayside entraining station. It made a very vivid impression on me: the cheering, shouting, singing march through the frosty sunlight, the tiny French town nestling at the end of its own valley, the quiet evening sky, the blue smoke lazily rising from the houses—these last things I remarked as we waited for the train to start. There was a buffet managed by two friendly ladies from Yorkshire, who doled out coffee and bread to the men. Then the troop-train—at least half a mile long—moved off very slowly, very cautiously, and, having proceeded about four miles, halted for as many hours. We slept along the seats. Once, about midnight, the train stopped on a bridge with a terrific jerk, and some French Territorial guards shouted incomprehensible observations from the road beneath. The morning, brilliantly fine, found us at Abbeville. And all day long we rolled on and on, moving, stopping, jolting. Now by the seaside, now by the sandhills about Calais, now through illimitable marshes, then through the ordinary undulating countryside, with its grey farms and green fields and venerable church towers, and at last among the flat, cold lands of Picardy. Nor was there any sign of war except an occasional Red Cross train and an uncommon military activity along the main road that ran beside the railway. Even at the rail-head ten miles from the Front there was no sound of guns, no particular stir in the air, except in the station yard where the three thousand troops detrained. It was about five o'clock, Sunday, and after dark. A guide led us through the narrow streets of the town of Merville, ill-lit and cobbled. We filed into a disused and dilapidated tobacco factory, where on the hard floor of lofts and storage-houses the men were to billet. It was a place of rats and shadows and creaking boards. Having made the necessary arrangements, Jarvis and I adjourned to our own billet in the house of a worthy citizen of the town. The old couple, wizened and bent and shy, having doubtless spent all their years in this backwater of civilisation until the war came, showed us politely to our rooms and beds. We slept snugly this night, but not before I had repaired to the headquarters of the Army Corps on a matter of urgency. Unlike the traditional headquarters of an army, the atmosphere of the little inn, before which a sentry stood and a red flag hung, was essentially tranquil. Only the sound of typewriters and the presence of a few waiting orderlies indicated that anything was astir. I was ushered before the General. Brisk and business-like, he was seated at a table, smoking a cigar. His Chief of Staff and aides-de-camp stood in front of the fire, doing likewise. All had just finished dinner. No time was wasted. My business finished, I went out into the dark street. Not a sound. A silvery moon shone down upon the little sleeping town. Could this be war, I asked myself, this calm and tranquil atmosphere? So puzzling, I went to bed.

Next morning found us lined along a road leading out of the town—a variegated column fifteen hundred strong, for at nine o'clock we were to be inspected by the General. He spoke a few words, and the column moved off, through a dense grey mist that hid the fields on either hand, on a fifteen-mile march to the Battalion. The highway was of *pavé* and trying to the feet. A Staff officer rode in front, and after an hour's trudging called a halt. The men were glad enough to fall out. It was their first march carrying packs and full weight of equipment. It was also my first march with full equipment, but I got through it better than I expected and found a friendly officer who took me into his billet and gave me food and a drink. But what a desolate country, such squalid people, such squalid straggling towns and tenements! Opposite the halting place was a house with a gaping hole in the roof where, a few days before, a German shell had burst. This was our first taste of the war. Henceforward many of the houses by the roadside were similarly damaged, albeit they seemed to be occupied; for besides soldiers, women and children swarmed in the streets. And this first impression of mine, the one and only impression, that of unutterable squalidity, was further borne out as we proceeded. They were so dingy, these towns, with their mud and their smoke-stains and their depraved-looking inhabitants. We halted once again in a dirty street. By now our limbs were aching and tired. Then, turning off along a lane, we struck out into the open country. Presently we came upon a line of guns—4·7's—cleverly concealed. The whole thing, the whole journey until we halted at about two o'clock in the afternoon before the farmhouse where the Staff of the Battalion was awaiting us, conveyed to the mind a sense of hopeless unreality. Surely this could not be a real war, I thought repeatedly. Surely this must be a dream, or an exhibition, or some kind of excursion, or a moving picture! Yet, no—it was war right enough—the trenches were only a mile away.

CHAPTER II

BILLETS AND THE FIRING LINE

I am writing this now in a farmhouse a mile from the German trenches. An occasional gun goes off, otherwise nothing comes out of the damp mist but the bark of a dog or the sound of our men chopping firewood outside. It is the strangest thing to see life running its normal course within a mile of the fighting line—children playing outside the cottages, peasants ploughing and threshing and so forth. Since our arrival yesterday the Battalion has come out of the trenches a little to the east of Sailly and we (also of the Second Battalion of the Twentieth Brigade of the Seventh Division) do not go in for four days. The rule is seven days in and seven days out. After that we may go into Divisional billets, which are really comfortable and outside shell-fire.

My Company Commander is a chap called Warner, who seems very decent. And, besides Jarvis and myself, there is a very pleasant fellow named Teddy Hulse. Seymour, whom I know slightly, is with us here too, but he has just gone on leave. Our farmhouse is well within range of the German guns, but I don't think they worry much about it. Warner has just been telling me of some things I shall want, and it appears I stand in need of gum-boots, a periscope, carriage candles, matches, a bottle of port, a plum cake and a box of cigarettes.

This afternoon we had an inspection by Heyworth, the Brigadier, who is a very efficient officer. The guns go on more or less all day. There is a battery of 7·7's close to this farm, and the German field guns reply. To-night I have to take a party to dig within a hundred yards of the German trenches, so shall probably hear something of them. I have got a foot a bit blistered owing to marching on the *pavé*, but feel otherwise as fit as a fiddle. There seems to be plenty to do here, even if one is in billets.

My brief visit to the trenches last night with my digging party was not very eventful. We started at five o'clock in the afternoon and got back at ten o'clock at night. Some of my men caught it from a Maxim gun, but no one was hit and only a few stray bullets came over, but it was quite exciting crawling down there and back. It seemed strange to be sitting within a hundred yards of the German lines and to hear them talking, shouting and singing and our people doing the same; big guns going intermittently all the time, with bursts of rifle-fire and a machine-gun tapping away at intervals. The Bosche snipers were also constantly cracking off, and every now and then we would see a star rocket shoot off in the distance. For a mile or two in view of the trenches everything is laid waste—ruined farms and great shell-pits in the ground. And very ghastly it all looks in the moonlight.

We go in the trenches to-morrow, Thursday, night for four days to relieve the First Grenadier's Battalion. Maurice Darby, a friend of my youth and incidentally a nephew of Sir George Arthur, is with them. Perhaps

I shall run into him. We come out on Monday night, March 1st, and in our turn go into Divisional billets some way back for a week, and then back to the trenches again. The weather has become miserable—cold and wet; this is the only similarity, it seems, between this spot and London.

I have never been so reluctant to leave a squalid place as I was this evening. How warmly the firelight flickered on the walls and beams of that wayside farm-kitchen in Picardy! How comfortable even the filthy farmyard looked amid its enclosing lofts and byres! And the two misshapen rooms where we billeted those four more or less peaceful days since Monday. Dirty they were and difficult and cavernous, yet to-night so enticing. Outside there had sprung up a little chilly evening wind when we ventured forth. But yesterday I should have sat by the window, reading. And to-night there lay before us the walk to the trenches, a long night's watching, four days and four nights in the firing-line.

We marched off.

Into a wintry sunset; the road yet muddy after recent rains; the dank fields lying cold and uninviting on either hand. Approaching the cross-roads, we quickened step, for were not they marked by the German artillery?

And of all the dreary places in all the dreary lands that I have seen I picture that group of wayside houses as the saddest. Always—except when the working-parties hurried by—an unnatural stillness reigned.

Roofless skeletons of houses and houses broken in a score of places; people creeping in and out, French peasants who cling pitifully to the relics of their homes; children peering out of the windows and doorways, too scared to play; heaps of ruins; and everywhere a great lonely emptiness.

We turned off into the fields. Yet the sunset was still in the sky, and it was too light to cross the open lands. We had to wait. The men smoked cigarettes and fell to talking after their inconsequent fashion about the prospects of the night, also of professional football, and —their suppers. Then darkness crept up and the sun dipped beyond the grey rim of the Flanders plain. It was twilight. We moved on across the ploughed fields. Not a sound, not a murmur of war. Until of a sudden we were in the road again, a road congested with troops. Battalion headquarters lay before us, and many transport wagons were unloading by the wayside. Long files of men in hoods and capes and heavy equipment, the rifle slung over the shoulder, moved slowly along towards the trenches. There were orderlies on horseback, sitting their horses like statues silhouetted against the evening sky.

We crawled forward presently at a snail's pace until clear of the congested trench-parties, then turned off to the left down a path, following a light ammunition railway. On the one hand were overhanging trees, on the other ghastly wrecks of houses. Soon we came to the little cemetery where our comrades lie amid the shell-pits and the ruined houses, under white wooden crosses. Nor could I pass by that spot, melancholy as it was, without recalling the company sergeant-major's sly humour. Never would he bring the nervous newly-joined subaltern down that way, I had heard, but he showed him with unction, with emphasis—and a twinkle in his eye—that little cemetery of nameless graves.

The occasional bullet pinging across our path told us how near we were to the trenches. Some desultory rifle-fire in front gave additional warning. Soon we were in the machine-gun zone and, stooping low, we hurried along the ditch beside the white strip of road, then across an open bit of ploughland towards the shelter of a parapet. Suddenly a machine-gun opened. We fell flat on our faces, and the bullets whistled overhead as the devilish thing swept round. But one man caught it and did not rise with us. Then we crept along behind the parapet which led rather steeply to a ruined barn. Here the troops in reserve were crouching over the fires they had kindled, cooking their supper. The fires cast a strange glare around. It was a place of shadows and passages and creeping armed men. The company whom we were to relieve filed out of the trenches and we filed in.

I placed my sentries. I laid down my pack and equipment in my dug-out. Carrying only my revolver, I walked along the line of the breastwork, noting here an improvement that had been made since my former very brief visit, and there a defect. Climbing the rear face of a little hill, I sat down behind the machine-gun emplacement, which was safe and a vantage-point. From there towards the enemy I could look across the plain.

And there you find me.

I see a wide and shadowy country. The moon is rising out of the calm night. A little wind whines and whispers among the sandbags. I see dimly a land of poplars and small trees (dwarf oaks), orchards, and plentiful willows. I see flat fields and ditches and stagnant water, and red farms whose roofs are gone, stark skeletons in the moonlight. I see broad flat spaces and then a ridge—the ridge of Aubers. Only the German lines are hidden from sight.

No sign of life. Silence and desolation reign. But here and there the faint glimmer of a fire indicates the presence of the enemy. Afar off, rockets, red and green and white, shoot up to the sky; star-shells bursting above our trenches cast their baleful light around. Strange twisted figures of trees stand out against the horizon. There is no sound but an occasional home-like mating-call of partridges in the fields and the peculiar laughing cry of the little speckled owl which here, as in England, dwells among the orchards. Creeping into the little den which I share with Warner, after a brief attempt at making things ship-shape, I fall asleep.

I woke this morning—it was my first awakening in the trenches—to hear the sizzling of bacon in a pan. A ray of light came streaming in through the opening of the dug-out. It was nine o'clock. Warner was still asleep, breathing regularly. I turned over and, according to a lifelong habit, indulged in a little leisurely contemplation previous to waking up properly. I remembered how infernally cold my feet had been in the early hours of the morning when I had crept in to sleep. But now they were warm and comfortable, wrapped around with empty sandbags and covered over with a rug and great-coat. The interior of the dug-out was moist and clammy. It was also exceedingly untidy. For the coverings and equipment of my companion and myself were strewn about the ground, grievously intermixed with straw, mud, newspapers, books, notebooks, and ration tins. The night before we had hastily rigged up little shelves, each in his corner, upon which we set those smaller things, such as matches and pencils, that are so apt to get lost, so that in parts there was a semblance of tidiness, but we had not been able to do much, for a candle stuck to a board by its own grease was the only illumination of our dug-out.

Then, while I was still contemplating, a face was pushed in through the dug-out opening, a hand prodded my lower extremities, and a voice said, "Breakfast is ready, sir." At the same moment *le capitaine* woke up. Smith, our faithful cook and my servant, began to pass in the food and the knives and the plates. First a plate of porridge, most welcome, and milk in a dark green bottle. This was followed by bread, and Belgian butter on a piece of paper, and marmalade from Piccadilly. Finally, steaming hot bacon and a poached egg on a plate. These we poised on our laps and ate voraciously. In fact, we didn't fare badly.

Feeling like nothing on earth, we didn't talk, but Warner read the *Westminster Gazette*, while I had a copy of the *Weekly Times*. Presently our invaluable Smith produced some of Warner's port, after drinking which we felt better, and one of us swore down the telephone for about a quarter of an hour, finding the field telegraph useful in more ways than one; letting it act as a kind of safety-valve for our humours. Disentangling myself by degrees from the rugs and the coats and the sandbags, I then crawled outside. There is a narrow passage-way under the front parapet between our own dug-out and that of the servants. Here Smith, and Warner's servant Walter, had lighted their fire, over which they crouched, eating their own breakfast.

I climbed over this, and turned to the right into the fort, where a number of men were sitting around smoking, mending their clothes, and cleaning their rifles. It was a sunshiny morning with a sharp little wind, and the country behind looked quite attractive with its fields and farms. There was no shooting or sound of war, since the Germans, barely eighty yards away, were doubtless as leisurely engaged as we. I exchanged a few words with the artillery observation N.C.O. and took a look through the periscope, which, however, disclosed nothing beyond the white facing of the enemy parapet showing here and there amid the irregularities of the ground. It was then about time to go down to the other end of the section held by the company, since in half an hour the Brigadier and C.O. were due to inspect it.

Being somewhat above six feet in height, I had to bend low as I passed down the line. In places, too, the breastwork is lower than in others, and there are often bits without any protection at all. The whole section, which is bordered at the further end by a road, is about five hundred yards long. At intervals of about one hundred and fifty yards there are "forts"—*i.e.* small walled-in areas of ground containing a machine-gun emplacement or observation post. I crept along rapidly from one to another of these, since it was not advisable to waste much time in between.

At one point there has not been an opportunity of building up sandbags, so hurdles have been put up instead, with the earth banked up behind them and a shallow ditch dug on the inside. There was more than one plank bridge to cross. About half-way along, after emerging from a muddy pit, the path dips down into a veritable maze of deep narrow trenches, boarded at the bottom, with numerous communication trenches running out from them. Here and there are open spaces where the fires are lit, and around these are the dug-outs, which made the place look like nothing so much as the exposed section of a rabbit-warren.

Through all these difficulties the Brigadier had to make his way—minus the gold lace, the red cap, and the Staff. For he, well known as a model of well-groomed smartness, was just like the rest of us, clad in gum-boots and an old uniform without a hat. At other times Heyworth has been known to ride horseback down the road to within a few hundred yards of the enemy, red cap, aide-de-camp, and all; and, as it happened, not a shot was fired. The inspection did not take long, and presently we were back again in the dug-out, making arrangements for to-night's work. Reports and diaries had to be written up, and there was much telephoning to headquarters concerning the strength of the working-parties about to be detailed. Then it was luncheon-time, which important event was preceded by an appetising whiff of cooking from the crackling fire outside.

Luncheon was followed by a long and deep sleep, which, however, was disturbed by the conversation of the guns. I woke up with a start to find the ground quaking with their detonation, while boom after boom proclaimed that an artillery bombardment was in progress. In the midst of it from the recesses of the next dug-out I could hear the business-like voice of the artillery N.C.O. reporting the result of each shot to his battery as it was shouted across to him by the observation officer with the periscope. Going outside, I learned that this affair had been in progress for an hour or more and that our own guns were just beginning to find the range of the enemy's fire-trench. Almost yard by yard the observation officer brought them down to it, until presently a shell evidently landed right on the trench, for the explosion was followed by a great upheaval of earth and stones, in the midst of which there sailed upward a German's trousers.

During this time the air whined and whistled with the passage of shells, and I felt almost surprised that I could not see them hurtling through the air. Desultory rifle-shots punctured this monotony of sound, while British aeroplanes came constantly circling and whirring overhead. It was not long, either, before the enemy shells began to burst not so far away, and the languid interest shown by the men in these proceedings was considerably livened when a shell landed on the parapet a couple of hundred yards away, knocked it down, and blew a number of sandbags sky-high, without, however, doing any more serious damage. The Germans were not really trying for us, but for our batteries farther back.

As the afternoon wore on I lost interest in this little display of temper by either side, and the next entertainment afforded me was the persistent efforts of an enterprising sniper to knock down the telephone-post above the dug-out. Probably he thought he had spotted an extra large periscope. It was amusing to hear the bullets pinging overhead and smacking or flattening themselves against the parapet while we ate our tea comfortably behind it. Nor did the sniper, persistent as he was hour after hour this afternoon, hit his mark. As dusk is now descending he is delaying further effort until to-morrow.

I have now had four days and nights in the trenches and seen, I suppose, nearly the whole gamut of war at its present stage. Except for the one man who was killed on our way in, I have had no casualties in my three forts, although our line has been constantly enfiladed by Bosche machine-gun fire.

Last night, it being Sunday, the Germans made a devil of a row with mouth-organs. I could hear them singing too—the Austrian National Anthem—all along my front. It was very strange seeing right away down the German lines and watching the heavy fighting far to the right—the glare and flash of the big guns, the shooting of star rockets, and the fires lighted along the German lines. Other times it would be very quiet and I could see the Germans (like ourselves) creeping about in the moonlight, building up their barbed wire, digging and so forth. And in a way I shall miss it, for to-day, it being the auspicious Monday, March 1st—as soon as it is dark—we move out of this mud into billets. All the morning the sun has shone placidly—and the majority of us slept—and this afternoon our guns began a concert which reached a crescendo about four o'clock. The enemy replied, but in a minor key, and it seemed rather doubtful whether either of us did the other any damage in particular. Then, as the bombardment was dying down, there arose a thunderstorm accompanied by lightning and mighty gusts of wind and rain, through all of which the guns boomed continuously. Such a crashing and rolling and booming one had never heard. The snipers and machine-guns all joined in, it was a blessed inferno, but we were all right behind our breastworks. Finally the setting sun peeped out upon a wet world, and we came swarming forth from our dug-outs and shelters like so many rabbits from their holes. It is packing-up time.

All the small litter that had accumulated during our days in the trenches we then threw upon the fires, the dug-outs were cleared of their contents, and the men began to get dressed. And what a collection of things some of them had—all their worldly goods! Some of them carried sandbags full of valued trifles, and others were decorated at every vantage so as greatly to resemble a Christmas-tree. Once ready, they formed up in file along the support trench, only the sentries remaining on the watch, and awaited the arrival of the relieving party.

Silence was enjoined—no smoking. Dusk had not long fallen when stealthy footsteps were heard approaching along the road. Presently the familiar muffled forms of soldiers appeared, each figure showing momentarily against the sky as it clambered into the trench. One by one they filed in and silently took their places alongside our men. When the sentries have been relieved and the incoming officer-in-charge has been shown the results of the work done on the trenches, wire entanglements, and parapets, we begin to move out in the same silent way. First along a deep ditch half-full of water, then behind a stout sandbag breastwork which presently crosses the road. Much encumbered with mud and weeds, in places it is a mere pathway. To-night we have the advantage of a deep blue gloaming, accompanied by a light veil of mist rising from the ground. Not a shot is fired, though everybody takes care to hurry along in small groups.

The fields lie dark and uninviting on either hand. The white skeleton of some ruined building which may have been a cottage or farmhouse stares out of the gathering darkness. The ground rises slightly, and presently we are at the cross-roads, where numerous bodies of troops, just relieved like ourselves from the trenches, are moving this way and that. Here the company is formed up and told off, while the remainder of the Battalion with the transport takes its place in the rear. As soon as possible the column moves off in fours, the men light their cigarettes and talk. It is now pitch dark. Little can be seen on either hand but a foot or so of mud. But suddenly, as we emerge from the houses on to higher ground, a great glare in the sky ahead confronts our eyes. In the midst of it, though far away, one can discern through the various obstacles of distance a suggestion of bright flames leaping upward.

Evidently it is a village burning, set alight no doubt by the bombardment of the German guns this afternoon. For they had been firing at long range, and it was hard to tell what, if not our batteries, their objective might be. As we advanced so the glare in the sky became broader and broader, and presently we could distinguish the bright spot of flame in the centre of it where the fire actually was.

At this moment we ran into a great body of troops. Halted along the road they were in column of route, long lines of infantry, guns and transport. As may be supposed, the narrow country byway and the crossroads further on were terribly congested, and it was all we could do to make any headway. Mounted orderlies were constantly riding down the column shouting to "Make way! make way!" while the Staff motor-cars and transport wagons occupied a great deal of space. We pushed on by fits and starts.

For we had run into part of the Canadian Division marching down to the trenches for the first time. To-night they would go into billets just behind the trenches and to-morrow take up the line.

All this busy scene, with its kaleidoscopic effects of bronzed faces—dark and almost Indian some of them—very strange dialects, horses, guns, vehicles, and men, was lit up magnificently by the glare of the burning village. I should think that Detaille or Verestchagin would rejoice could they have recorded such scenes as these, the little incidental cameos of war. They would have painted the faces half-turned, showing the full and rounded profile so typical of the Canadians; the smiling faces, the faces set and grim, the tired, mud-stained faces in endless succession from front to rear; they would have made a feature, perhaps, of the men on horseback whose figures—the rifle slung across the back, the collar of the great-coat turned up—silhouetted picturesquely against the red glare on the horizon; they would have shown the artillery-men grouped around their guns, and the long wet streaks in the muddy road, the tall upright poplars here and there, and beyond all the brilliant spot of flame where the homes of the peasantry burned.

It is a picture, I am sure, with an historic significance not soon to be forgotten, although at the time there is much cursing among the soldiers on account of the delay in our journey "home." "Hullo! kiddo," say the Canadians, and much chaff passes between the two bodies of men. By degrees we thread our way through the columns of troops which are converging from various roads, and then are held up by an almost interminable train of motor-lorries, whose brilliant head-lights dazzle the eyes. Once beyond these, we swing along again, and the men break into their favourite marching songs:

"Who's Your Lady Friend?" the song about the high road and the low road, "On the Mississippi," and so forth, alternating with the eternal question, "Are we downhearted?" and the inevitable answer, "No." Always ahead of us, nearer and nearer, beckons the burning village, so close now that we seem to be walking into it, until presently we turn sharp to our right down a side-road. We have come four miles.

Half a dozen friendly pipers from a Highland regiment come out from their billets playing a complimentary air on their bagpipes; and so we march into supper—and bed.

The morning light comes filtering in through the closed shutters of the farmhouse where we are billeted. And Walter, in the next room, is heard saying to his confederate Smith, "We'd better wake them up, 'adn't we?" and Smith is heard to reply, "Yes, or there'll be trouble." Now, Smith is a rough, burly fellow, who has a habit of violently jogging one's elbow when half asleep and whispering in his hoarse way, "Time to get up, sir." The usual reply to which is, "For Heaven's sake, go and kill yourself." Walter, on the other hand—he has been a valet—is the sort of man who goes quietly about his business and announces it is time to bestir just three minutes before the hour for parade. Good fellows as they are—and, as servants, none better—they contrive to do some extraordinary things. When, the other night in the trenches in the early hours, I had to transfer to a new dug-out at the farther end of the line,

Smith and Walter found me. Through the bright moonlight they came, an unmistakable mark for the German bullets, plodding happily along together, Walter carrying his friend's pots and pans and cooking apparatus, Smith burdened with several newspapers, a brown-paper parcel, a cake, a bottle of gin, a blanket, and a rifle. So they had been wandering about, jumping ditches, climbing fences, and struggling through the trenches, at imminent risk to life and limb, until—as usual—they found their destination in the end.

But now let me say a little more about Warner, with whom I live and mess. He is my kennel companion—for only so can one describe it—and at the present moment he is washing himself in a little canvas pail. He is naked to the waist, his skin being very white, like a woman's, and he has a childish, pink face. His braces hang loose by his sides. He is swearing quietly to himself because it is very cold—and no one has a mightier vocabulary. A peculiarly urbane and agreeable young man, there is none more gallant or more capable. He does not "tell people off"; he does not fuss; but he gets things done. Which is the highest tribute one can pay to a soldier. In peace-time he had been an A.D.C. or some such *attaché* to the Aberdeens.

Presently together—having breakfasted—at an inconveniently square table—we go out to the company parade, which happens in an orchard. It is a lovely morning. The brilliant sunshine makes even the sad land look fair and almost attractive. Not a sound comes from the direction of the trenches, though an aeroplane—one of our own—is slowly buzzing its way across the sky. The singing of innumerable larks is the only other sound. We go round the billets and walk about for a time, feeling more like exceptionally peaceable farmers than soldiers on active service. How pleasant it is after the great strain of the trenches! The courtyard of this French farm presents a scene sufficiently typical of the war in the West.

The British soldier is lounging about with all his accustomed *négligé*, the stump of a cigarette in his mouth; the cocks and hens (with crested heads) and one or two fat black pigs are scratching and burrowing in the somewhat pungent and very plentiful manure of the farmyard. *Madame*, wizened and old, with two rubicund daughters, is heavily committed in the matter of washing linen outside the kitchen door. *Monsieur le père*, who has an imperial and a short white pipe which he never ceases to smoke, leans contemplatively on the door of a cowhouse regarding the unwonted scene. Who would think that the opposing lines of trenches, locked together in the grim death struggle, are so near? Yet hardly has the thought occurred when in the middle distance a gun booms ominously.

After transacting certain business with the company sergeant-major, a square, thick-set man with a non-committal manner and a gruff voice, we proceed to battalion headquarters, first, however, inspecting the billets of the men in lofts, barns, and cow-byres. On the whole they are very comfortable, bedded down on dry straw, with a bundle of hay for head-rest. At battalion headquarters orders are transacted, punishments for misdemeanours awarded, and future operations, either in or out of the trenches, discussed in detail by the Commanding Officer, the Adjutant, and the company officers. After which we go our several ways to the midday meal. Our own billet is about half a mile distant down a long, straight bit of road, bordered on either hand by flat fields and ditches, willows and dwarf oaks. There is no traffic on the road but an occasional wagon rattling past. Only a few groups of gunners are visible here and there. The one notable sound is the busy humming of a threshing-machine at the neighbouring farm.

A midday meal, more ample than elegant, awaits us: beefsteak, with bacon and many potatoes, steaming hot; slices of stout plum cake sent from home—for this is pudding ready-made; and much ration bread with very white Belgian butter and jam. And through the half-open doorway we catch a glimpse as follows: the worthy Smith and his crony Walter are seated on biscuit-boxes by the fireside, balancing their cheese on the edge of their knives. They are surrounded by the whole French family—*père et mère et filles*—from whom frequently come peals of laughter at the sallies perpetrated by our faithful satellites in Glasgow–Cockney *parlez-vous*. And, truth to tell, the good people never cease to laugh and jest though the enemy are at their very gates. Which is the way of their country. Nor can I write that the Germans behaved badly when billeted here; neither was it otherwise the case in the other billets known to me. First in September last year came the Uhlans to this wayside farmhouse; and later a detachment of Hussars. They paid for everything they took and all behaved respectfully. Which is one of the few things I have heard so far to the credit of our enemies.

After luncheon there is a musketry parade, and afterwards we stroll down to a field to watch a football match. The battalion team is playing an artillery eleven. Everybody is there to watch the game: much excitement. No one notices the incessant boom of the German guns and the scream and the bang of their shells, which are exploding as regularly as clockwork around a farmstead not three hundred yards away, until attention is momentarily distracted by a shell bursting unmistakably in the very next field. Then someone bethinks himself of the threshing-machine, which, sending up a column of black smoke, offers an ideal target to the German artillery. At the same time our own guns take up the challenge, and the game of football goes calmly on beneath an unending procession of Jack Johnsons. So accustomed is everybody to this comparatively harmless demonstration that no one takes the smallest interest in it until a shell chances to crash the roof of the little inn which stands at the cross-roads near by.

It seems advisable to go home to tea. A busy evening awaits us. A great pile of at least two hundred letters have to be censored. Each must be glanced through before being officially stamped. This, though a privilege, is one of the most onerous (and tiresome) duties of company officers at the front. But Seymour is just back from leave to help us. Meanwhile the Germans have ceased shelling, as have our own guns, and all is quiet outside. We work by the light of candles thrust into the necks of empty bottles. Presently the post arrives—the greatest event of this and every day—and it has to be answered. Writing letters home is a pleasure second only to that of receiving them. Also the English newspapers come to hand. And there is a bottle of port done up tantalisingly in straw, and a new cake, not to mention a beautiful boneless chicken in a glass case. Perhaps the thought is a little degrading—I mean that one lives for one's stomach these days, and the invariable source of quarrel between man and his friend is that the latter has better food or more of it!

After dinner the men have a concert in the big barn. There they all gather, serried masses of them, lying on the piles of straw and hay, ranged along the beams, and squatting in rows upon the floor. And Jock, who has a concertina, performs upon it; and Bill, who is a bit of a wag, sings funny songs; and Alf provides a sentimental ditty (chiefly about the girl he left behind him); while Warner tells the most outrageous stories in the drollest manner possible; and everybody smokes and claps and jests and roars to their heart's content. So that for this brief hour we all forget the war—which, I verily believe, is the chief ambition of every honest soldier at the front.

What is this?

"Fall in! . . . Sergeant-Major!"

Although we have been here only a day we are bound for new billets eight miles away at Vieux Berquin, to be in Army Corps reserve probably for a week, after which we may move anywhere. Why is this? Nobody knows.

"Hurry up there. Hurry up."

About a mile away there is a motor-lorry burning. It lights up the whole countryside.

The march late last night was rather trying, as none of us were in much condition for that sort of thing. We are in quite comfortable billets in a farmhouse by the road, and where we are there is something definitely in the wind, probably a big attack. There are masses of troops about. And two new officers have arrived. We have to mess by companies, such is the congestion.

I have just seen the Prince of Wales riding down the road on his way from General Headquarters.

The weather has turned very nasty—cold and wet—so I suppose we are in for a bad time.

We move again this afternoon, Sunday, March 7th, (having been here but five days) to Estaires, a town about five miles away—into other billets!—and then back into the trenches, I am afraid, to-morrow, Monday, night; a different part of the line though from where we were before. It is a great nuisance, as since late Tuesday night we have been in very comfortable billets. We have done little here except clean up and practise attacks and censor letters. Yesterday afternoon I walked about a mile over to the First Grenadiers' billets and saw Maurice Darby. He seemed very fit and jovial and very much alive.

I wonder how much longer this war is going to last.

Everyone who has been out here above a week or two is sick to death of it and praying for the end, and I am not surprised.

Even if the billets are good, the country, the towns, and the people here in Artois are the most miserable I have ever struck. The countryside is something like Cambridgeshire or Essex, but infinitely worse. In general the houses are flimsy, rotten things.

CHAPTER III

NEUVE CHAPELLE

At five o'clock of a wintry morning, that of March 10th, 1915, our war-stained Battalion left its billets at Estaires, where we had rested some three days. It was not yet light. Only the grey opaqueness of the sky suggested the coming of daylight, which presently would filter through the streets and between the shutters of the houses.

Along those streets, among the houses, an icy little north-east wind whined and whispered. Snowflakes drifted down, large and slow, like ghosts of white birds. Snow lay thinly upon the roof-tops, upon the pavements, upon the surface of the road. Men's feet were silent as they moved about. There were no lights but the occasional flash of an electric torch and the beam which shot out from the half-open door of some emptying billet. There were no sounds but the muffled thump of gloved hands sharply brought together, an occasional low exclamation, an occasional query in the darkness.

Lines of men stretched dimly along the side of the road. Mysterious shapes they were in the dim light of dawn, mysterious, indefinite. Many wore hoods and all wore greatcoats with full weight of equipment—the pack bulking upon the back, the rifle slung over the shoulder. Here and there a mounted orderly sat like a statue, his figure and horse outlined against the gradually lightening sky. Now and then a motor-cyclist, crouching low and heavily burdened, rattled past over the *pavé*. Farther down the road long lines of transport could be discerned—tarpaulin-covered wagons, a machine-gun section, numerous artillery limbers.

The growing daylight revealed these things. So did the growing daylight reveal a curious stir and movement in those streets of silent houses. Now a sharp low word of command, now the champing of bits or the stamp of hoofs where the Brigadier's horses were awaiting him—always the erratic movement of troops which were trying by degrees to make their way out of the town. "Form fours! Right! By the right, quick march!"

The column moved slowly off, only to halt presently at the market-place, in front of the red-brick, artificial-looking French church, where there was a great congestion of transport and artillery. A long pause, while men stamped their feet and clapped their hands for warmth. Then on again along the main *pavé* road. Now the snowflakes had ceased, and the clear steely light of morning grew in the streets. Just as in London or Paris workmen and market-women were doubtless creeping along the pavements even at this hour, so here within a few miles of the guns which were soon to thunder in deadly earnest they were going to their work in peaked caps and blue blouses, the women's heads covered with coloured shawls. Many who would otherwise be in bed are at their windows or doors, curious and rather frightened at the tramping of so many feet.

Past the market-place and the brewery and the rows of insubstantial-looking red-brick houses, with their ornamented façades and childish front-doors and shutters—so across a bridge which spans a sluggish, dirty stream. Then the long column winds away to the right along a rough track, inches deep in mud, which leads across waste land in the rear of a factory. Here are many slag-heaps, acres of black soil and rubbish-heaps, as in the outskirts of Black-Country towns. Beyond them is an open space apparently designed by Nature as a military-exercise ground, for the expanse is unbroken, save by a fence of wire-netting which divides it in half. All around are tall chimneys of red-brick factories.

An entire brigade, including the extra Territorial Battalion, is assembled here; namely ourselves, the First Grenadiers, the Gordon Highlanders, and the Border Regiment. The men are drawn up in close column by Battalions for inspection by the Brigadier, who, with his Brigade-Major and Aide-de-Camp, trots down the lines. Orders rattle out in quick succession. "Stand easy! Pile arms! Packs off!" The men take off their equipment, lay it down, and sit upon their packs. The first refuge of the Tommy is his packet of cigarettes, the second his rations. Everywhere the rank-and-file lie about smoking and eating. The officers, meanwhile, grouped around their Battalion Commanders, are deeply engaged in studying and comparing maps. Here one observes an animated discussion, there a silent, painstaking inquisition, whilst yonder a lively group of subalterns is laughing and joking.

But for the hour and the surroundings one would say the assembly had a sort of garden-party air about it. And just as at some social affair an embarrassing silence often follows a burst of conversation, so now of a sudden everybody stops talking at once. All heads are turned the same way. Everybody listens. A low thunderous roll can be heard, punctured distantly by the bang-boom, boom-bang of innumerable guns. Somewhere beyond that low fringe of trees which tantalisingly borders the horizon the great bombardment of Neuve Chapelle has begun. Nothing can be seen, only that low furious mutter trembles along the horizon. Yet the conflagration spreads, and batteries nearer at hand begin to bang and boom, so that now and again one may glimpse a pale flash of fire against the grey morning sky.

We have been here nearly three hours and it is just after 7.30. The music has begun to the minute. Aeroplanes appear swiftly from all quarters, circling, whirring, droning in the sky.

Suddenly the familiar whistle of a big shell causes everybody to look up. Screaming through the air, it lands with a crash in a piece of waste land close to one of the tall chimneys. No harm is done, but are there more to follow? With a whole brigade massed in the open this is a serious question. Orders are immediately given to cut down the wire-netting which crosses and bisects the field, in order to give the troops a chance of scattering if a proper shelling begins. Those having wire-cutters speedily get to work, but nothing further eventuates.

On the contrary, there is a long and tedious and anxious wait. One munches chocolate and smokes cigarettes, feeling the while that these moments are big with fate for all of us here, and for all those thousands out there in ditches and trenches, along roads and behind hedges, who, like ourselves, are waiting to enter the battle which is now beginning. There is no news. Once the leading battalion moves off, only to come back again in a few minutes owing to the congestion of troops on the narrow roads in front. The regiments in the van have not moved out to attack. Sitting and waiting is the hardest thing of all in anxious times.

The guns mutter and roll, now close at hand, and now faint. It is a misty morning and the wind is blowing away from us; moreover, the country is dead flat, so that it is impossible to judge what may be occurring. All sorts of pictures rise to the mind: one can imagine the Indians, far away to the right, swarming out of their trenches, racing across the open fields, and jumping in with the bayonet quickly and silently—

"Packs on!"

"Get ready to move off!"

It is between 9 and 10 a.m. We march off in column of route and in rear of the Gordons and the Borders, the Grenadiers being behind. We are three miles from Estaires, and we march another three miles along narrow roads. Soon we come upon a dead straight *pavé* road stretching ahead between lines of poplars. The surface is all greasy after the rains, the mud mashed up by the feet of thousands. We march along this highway—it leads to Armentières—towards the sound of the guns. Orderlies and pioneer officers on bicycles are very numerous.

At the cross-roads a red-capped Staff officer is sitting on horseback by the roadside. The message he gives to us as we pass is that the first two lines of German trenches have been taken with slight loss. A little later another "red-cap" rides down the column on a bicycle, giving the news that the first three lines have been captured. This cheers the soldiers immensely, and, after the manner of his kind, Private Thomas Atkins immediately begins romancing about the quarters he will occupy in Berlin next week; for he is ingenuously under the impression that success here means an early end to the war. Progress is somewhat slow, as the road is alive with troops and movement of all kinds. Orderlies on horseback and bicycles dash past, great grey Staff motor-cars hoot their way imperiously through the mass of men, transport-wagons and Red Cross motor-ambulances in various stages of mechanical difficulty help to block the road.

All the wayside cottages and farmhouses have their quota of troops, who are awaiting their turn to move up to the firing-line. Presently we wheel off into a labyrinth of lanes winding this way and that, and now we are within effective range of the German artillery. Already this morning one section of the road which runs parallel to our front has been liberally shelled, and, as a precaution therefore, we move in artillery formation across the fields. Safely on the road again, the thunder of the guns seems very close.

Right and left as we pass them—concealed as they

are behind hedgerows, in orchards and farmyards—howitzer batteries can be seen firing furiously: a flash, a boom, a recoil, and the little gunners—looking at a distance like so many busy insects—rush forward to re-charge their guns. There they are, with their shirt-sleeves rolled up and braces hanging loose, working like demons at the smoking breeches.

Now we turn aside into a sheltered meadow by a farmstead. Packs are taken off, arms piled, and the men sit down for a rest, since we are likely to remain here some time.

It is now a mild, sunny morning, and the chill wind has gone down. With all the sounds of war and death at hand, the countryside looks peaceful enough. Two fields away a peasant is ploughing stolidly, heedless of the shells which now and again scream over his head. The greatest battle in the world's history may be raging a mile and a half away, but that is no reason why he should not finish his spring ploughing. Near by a little stream eddies through reeds and water-plants, making tinkling music, and its sunny banks are agreeably warm. Skylarks rise and sing not less vigorously, not less merrily than on any quiet morning of an English spring-time, though their outpourings are drowned at times in the whirr and buzz of circling aeroplanes.

The first tangible indications of the battle are the wounded men of the Twenty-first Brigade who have captured the German front-line trenches. They now come trickling back along the road. Bloody heads and hands roughly bandaged for the most part; albeit, now and then a still figure on a stretcher with chalky, quiet face tells a sadder story. And they are not in the least cheerful or boastful, as London daily newspapers delight to depict the wounded Tommy; but rather woebegone and very subdued.

"It was hell," they remark solemnly—for where is the sense of pretending that a common mortal feels heroic on coming out of a bloody holocaust?

And presently there comes a procession of German prisoners marching between French Territorials—fine great men of the Prussian Guard, very stolid and expressionless (although a few looked scared), with coarse, typically Teuton faces. There are smaller fry, too, Saxons and Alsatians, rather untidy and unsoldier-like, and looking with no great favour upon their comrades, the Prussians. Yet these Alsatians are the more intelligent, speaking excellent French, in which language they are heard to disparage their officers: they are townsmen, whilst the Prussians are ignorant peasants. One and all admit the completeness of the surprise, to which, indeed, their lack of accoutrements and general disorder bear testimony. Nor would it be far wrong to say that every man-jack of them is delighted to be a prisoner. In one place, I hear, they tried their rotten white-flag truce, but everywhere else were only too glad to surrender.

The morning wears on. Sitting on the sunny bank by the roadside, we watch the aeroplanes, French and English, ceaselessly circling overhead and journeying to and fro. They are like kites or hawks diligently observing their prey. Suddenly a whistling shriek rends the air. We look up instinctively, expecting a

16-in. shell. But no! We are petrified. We catch one glimpse of an aeroplane, already buckled and crumpling, diving to earth from about a thousand feet—then it is gone behind the trees. It is smashed to matchwood, and the two poor chaps in it, Irving and Morgan, are knocked about in a most awful way. They have been hit by a shell from one of our guns and have fallen like a stone.

Nor is it long before another aeroplane descends safely, but by a hair's breadth. The petrol tank has a hole large enough to put your arm in. All the way from La Bassée, where the German shrapnel had burst around it for half an hour on end, it had been leaking furiously. The two flying-men, looking particularly cheerful in their leathern garments and headgear, seemed to treat the whole matter as a joke.

All this time the batteries in the orchards, enclosures, and farmyards just behind had never ceased to boom and bang. Again and again the squat black howitzers peeping from their screen of leaves belch forth flame, jerk up their heads, and are immediately surrounded each by their little crowd of attendant gunners.

It is now nearly two o'clock. We eat our chocolate rations and a few sandwiches. No more news comes through, no more prisoners or wounded. But for the ammunition-limbers which constantly race along the road at breakneck speed to replenish their batteries, nothing in particular happens. Only the farmhouse near by is made the mark of the German guns, and mild interest is aroused when a shell lands on the roof and sets the thatch afire. Just at this juncture, however, word arrives to move down into the reserve trenches, newly dug. So far only an occasional German shell has come our way, but now we get a taste of them. Immediately behind us the 6-in. howitzer battery pops off regularly every three minutes, as on our right and left do field-gun batteries and behind them 9·2's. There are at least three hundred guns on our front of three miles. Every few minutes comes the scream of German lyddite or shrapnel, which bursts amid yellow and white smoke in the next field. I cannot describe the din and the crash and the smash. It is generally considered the greatest artillery show of the war, and I almost pity the wretched Germans. We are snugly ensconced in our trenches. Lying down at the bottom to escape the chilly wind, we get some sleep.

Meanwhile the men roam about the orchard gathering dry wood and sticks, with which they light their fires and crouch close to them. We, too, light a fire in the alcove of the trench and bivouac. Soon there is much crackling. The inestimable Smith, who has a genius for making tea, produces a tin cup and pannikin from his mess-tin, and presently we are quite comfortable sitting round waiting for the expected summons.

Towards evening the guns die away, and we stand to arms most of the night expecting to attack or be attacked at any moment. But no order comes. By the light of my electric torch I see Maurice Darby for a moment and we exchange greetings. Apart from the star rockets and searchlights and flares which light up the sky everything is quite quiet.

At 4 a.m. (March the 11th) orders come to move in half an hour.

As it is gradually getting light the Battalion advances. At a wayside farmhouse, which for the nonce is Brigade Headquarters, it halts. A bright beam of light shooting out from the doorway discloses the files of men, heavily burdened with great-coats, packs, haversacks, water-bottles, entrenching tools, and equipment. Strange figures they look in the dim light. Orderlies with steaming horses and one or two motor-cyclists are waiting outside. A long conference takes place between Staff Officers, the Commanding Officer, and the Adjutant.

We move on. We pass our old trenches. We leave the road and begin to follow a light ammunition rail way across fields. Eastward, the dawn breaks in streaks of ashy grey, shedding upon the countryside a cold and cheerless light. Many were there who looked upon daybreak for the last time. Not a word was spoken. It was all a man could do to pick his way along the narrow track on either side of which was liquid mud. Now and again we would meet parties of weary Highlanders trudging back from the firing-line for a well-earned rest. Presently in the distance a gun boomed. Close at hand another answered. Then one by one they took it up along the line behind. The grim business of our day had begun.

As the light grew, bullets began to whizz and hum above our heads. First occasionally, then increasingly, until the air sang with them. Quite close now in front there was a sudden little burst of rifle-fire. Across the open field we found ourselves in a road protected by a stout breastwork, occupied by the East Lancashire Regiment in reserve, and fairly swarming with troops. The question now was how to find cover for the whole Battalion. For already there was considerable congestion. Eventually this was done by splitting up the companies on either side of a gap in the line of sandbags through which bullets constantly whistled. My half-company was wedged together on one side of this dangerous gap. It was a ticklish business crossing, and we began to lose men.

Thereupon followed a weary hour's wait. It was six o'clock. Orders had come to attack at seven. The first thing to do was to provide for the inner man. No one had had breakfast—there had been no time for that. So the men lie about eating their rations and smoking. Some take off their great-coats and equipment, folding the former away in the pack; some clean their rifles and bayonets; some talk and laugh together over breakfast. The Lancashire men, who occupy the best place under the parapet of the trench, are doing likewise. And curious it is to hear at this odd moment in this odd place the intermingling of English dialects, Glasgow and Manchester, the burr of Devon, and the cockney Territorials' nasal twang. The anticipation is trying. We are ordered to advance in line of platoons. Right flank (my company) leading; Seymour on my right commanding one half-company, Warner in rear.

Very soon the Germans get busy. First one shell and then another hurtles across and bursts around a half-ruined, red-brick farmstead which stands beside the road. Soon they follow each other in regular succession minute by minute, now in front of the breastwork and now behind. Men walking along the road sink down beside it suddenly, whimpering like children, holding the head or clasping the limbs with their hands. Splinters and shrapnel bullets fly in all directions. The closer to the breastwork one is, so much the safer.

Seven o'clock approaches. Word comes that the attack on the right has been launched. Word is passed down to get ready. Officers load their revolvers and button their tunics across the throat. Platoons are marshalled together and told off. "Fix bayonets!" A cold, rasping sound, and six hundred blades flash in the morning sunlight.

"Move to the right in file!" "Right turn!" "Quick march!" The orders follow each other in quick succession. Number one company leads the way along the shell-stricken road. A lane branches off to the left; abutting upon it is a maze of deep, disused trenches. The Commanding Officer and Adjutant are here, uttering last words of encouragement to the men as they file into them. Knee-deep in mud and water they are, with planks laid along the bottom here and there to afford a better footing. At the end of the winding passages we halt, awaiting the final word. The order, when it comes, is short and simple: "Advance 95 degrees left."

Company officers blow their whistles and the whole front line swarms through the gaps in the sandbag breastwork and rushes pell-mell across a hundred yards of open ground, pitted with holes, and obstructed with loose strands of barbed wire. Directly we get out in the open we come under very heavy rifle-fire and shrapnel. Bullets sing and splutter merrily in all directions. Once across that open stretch we are in the first line of German trenches. Already they have been reversed by our infantry, though the trench is shallow and the breastwork low. Indeed, the crush of troops in this section is altogether too great. Men cannot obtain shelter from the ceaseless stream of bullets. Some even have to crouch down on the top of the ground. A strapping fellow topples forward groaning into the trench, his hands clasped to his forehead, from which the blood pours. Another rolls quietly over on his side—stone dead. The lad next to me, virile and strong a moment ago, now lies feebly moaning, shot through the body. Two or three others, variously wounded, sit, half-conscious, with their backs against the parapet.

And we have seen out only five minutes!

We can only advance in short rushes, taking cover wherever possible, and it is impossible to keep the formation. We are about half a mile west of Neuve Chapelle, and the country is absolutely open, only slight depressions here and there.

It is time for another rush. Up we clamber again, dive one by one under a loose strand of wire and stream diagonally in batches across an enclosure, men following officers as best they can. The air whistles, nay, tingles with bullets, and it is with a feeling more of surprise than anything that after each rush one reaches the other side. We find another breastwork similarly crowded with men, but better protected than the last. For the ground in front has been blown into a huge mound by the action of the British shells, and this provides adequate shelter. The mound must be at least forty feet high. Beneath it the soil has been hollowed and scarred and rent into a great cavity—a pit of horror indescribable. Here in some vast explosion all the refuse, all the material of the neighbouring trenches seems to have fallen. Many German dead are there, grey and bloody, amid the upturned earth; by itself lies the body of a British soldier, stark and stiff, the face covered, doubtless by some comrade's hand, with a piece of white tarpaulin; the trivial things of life are there—biscuit-tins, scraps of food, hand-mirrors, the trivial things men carry in their pockets. And everywhere litter of equipment—German helmets, with the golden eagle emblazoned on the front, German caps and accoutrements, rifles, clips of cartridges, pistols, and weapons of all kinds. The tradition of blood and iron has found its fitting consummation in this one place.

Through this pit we clamber and up the mound beyond; then dart along a kind of ridge. A small river or large ditch of stagnant water is bridged at one place by a plank which has broken down. It is no time to hesitate. The only thing to do is to plunge in and somehow stagger across with the filthy, brackish, greenish water lapping one's chin. Rifle and bayonet, already clogged with mud, are rendered useless. On the further bank lies a wounded Grenadier officer attended by his sergeant. The country is now dead flat and open, the enemy cannot be more than three hundred yards distant. A broad stretch of ploughed field, heavy with recent rains, has to be crossed. Men fall right and left, prostrate khaki figures dot the ground in all directions. The crackle of rifle-fire freshens, the whole air hums with bullets. Burdened with our packs and weight of equipment, we can only muster a jog-trot in such heavy going. Many prefer to crawl over the ground on all fours, though this little advantages them; some pause for breath in the shell-holes, others lie down in the open.

On the far side of the ploughed field is a shallow depression in the ground. Here, the only available cover, are disposed a number of troops of various companies and regiments. Immediately in front, not one hundred and fifty yards away, is a group of buildings surmounted by a tall, red-brick chimney—a landmark in all that countryside—known as the Moulin du Piétre. It looks more like a mine in one of our own colliery districts than a mill. It fairly bristles with rifles and machine-guns. The hail of bullets above our heads increases. We flatten our faces in the muddy ground and lie there for three solid hours under a hell fire that seems to come from every side but one. Shrapnel bursts as regularly as clockwork within twenty or thirty yards and scatters earth over one every time.

Behind us the rear companies of the Battalion are still advancing. They come on in groups and batches in widely extended order. Meanwhile, we lie down in a long, irregular line which grows thicker, thus affording a better mark for the enemy's riflemen and artillery. So, presently, the order comes for two platoons to advance about a hundred yards to a line of temporary breastworks and rejoin the Grenadiers who are ahead. We show our heads and the bullets begin to fly as thick as hail.

I had hardly got to my feet and was jumping over a ditch when I was hit in the left leg and took an unceremonious toss down the bank. It hurt a bit for a time, but Warner and Seymour were moving up with me, so there was no confusion among the men. Five minutes later Seymour, as I shortly afterwards learned, got a shrapnel bullet through the head and collapsed, but by then our tide had passed on, out of my sight. My thigh hurt me in such a way that I could not move for at least two hours. Nor, indeed, dared I do so. For in the mill and its group of adjacent buildings only that bare hundred and fifty yards away the enemy still swarmed.

So I lay on my face motionless, listening to the sounds of the battle. They were so numerous that I cannot enumerate them all. It was the shrapnel which caused the greatest dread. How narrowly it whizzed overhead, to burst about thirty yards behind with a deafening bang and a flash of fire followed by the sing-sing of many bullets which buried themselves in the ground. Surely none could escape! The whole sky was dotted with the black smoke of high explosives and the yellow puffs of lyddite, each with its flash of flame. The air stank of powder and the fumes of sulphur.

More terrible—not to be forgotten—were the salvoes of the German batteries close in front, which fired almost together every three minutes. Boom-boom-boom-boom—they threatened to burst the brain, they caused a racking headache, these terrible tornadoes of sound. The machine-gun and the rifle-fire were as nothing after these. The rat-tat-tat, the clack-clack, the ping-ping sent their messages well overhead to the trenches behind and the still-advancing troops. Much other noise came to puzzle the ears, to weary the brain: the faint shouting of men, the clink-clink of the entrenching-tools as soldiers dug themselves in, the great hollow explosions which resounded afar off amid the ruins of Aubers and Neuve Chapelle.

And the groans, the moans, the crying of those who lay around!

I started to crawl back. The dressing-station was at least a mile away, but things seemed quieter. I crawled over the ground ever so slowly, for those riflemen in the mill were doubtless watching. The ploughed field seemed interminable—I could not see the breastwork on the other side, and the only landmarks were the dead and wounded men who lay at intervals along the direction of advance. Now the supports had ceased to come up. Yet suddenly, as happens in modern fighting, the combatants took inspiration, the battle burst forth afresh. One above another common shells and shrapnel exploded above and beside me, earth fell about my ears, bullets tingled past them. Flash after flash, as of lightning, dazzled my eyes. I was barely half-way across. Creeping into a deep shell-hole, I flattened my face. Close behind the German howitzer double-battery boomed shatteringly. Close ahead the firing of our own guns was so swift, so furious, as to be one continuous roar. Also the rifle-fire freshened along the whole front—it was as though some great dry wood-pile had been newly kindled. The air sang songs with the passage of the shells, the earth trembled under the detonation of such huge guns as had never been used before—shriek and roar, boom and bang and crackle.

For half an hour I lay there, in company with a dead man, thinking the end of all things had come.

But like some gust of human passion the holocaust spent itself at last. And I, leaving my Burberry, crawled on among the shell-pits and the relics of the soldiery, the rifles, the caps, and the helmets, the emptyings of pockets, the equipment and the haver-sacks, the wasted rounds of ammunition, the revolvers, and the scraps of food. Past many an upturned waxen face and shreds of men where shells had done their work—and blood. A head showed itself above the rim of a shell-hole. "Stop, sir," it said; "give me your pack. I'll keep it for you. You'll never carry it all the way." I did not like the face or the voice. I had heard strange tales. There was a marked map in my pack. I crawled on.

And found Grant presently, laying on his back. Poor Grant—he, so weathered and tough, so used to fighting, so sure with the rifle, solid and stolid, so able as sniper or scout! A bullet through the chest had left him in agony. And close at hand the unknown doctor from the Scots Fusiliers, who, without summons, had doubled across the shell-swept field to tend our wounded only himself to be shot through the body as he knelt beside them.

At last the friendly wall of sandbags is in sight, behind which our supports are sheltering. A deep and broad ditch or, rather, small stream of filthy water runs in front of this. Only at one place is it crossed by a single plank, all slippery, all slithery. Astride it, almost at right angles, blocking the way, lies the body of an English soldier. I make more than one attempt to cross. I slide to this side and that, for the plank is very narrow. My situation is precarious and painful, with the stinking muddy water beneath and the board bending under my weight. And there is the obstacle at the end. But at the moment some brawny lad extends a hand from behind the breastwork and drags me within its shelter by main force. I find three officers of the Devon regiment bunched up together under the parapet. After a rest to recover breath, I pull myself along the line of sandbags, through the mud, which in places is inches deep. Wounded men lie at intervals propped against the breastwork, some unconscious, some nursing heads or limbs, while a couple of doctors and stretcher-bearers are busily engaged attending to them as quickly as may be.

I leave the breastwork behind, having been directed towards the dressing-station, and with frequent pauses for breath cross another field.

I find myself in an orchard.

It is very quiet here, save for the occasional shells

which whistle overhead. Actually I can hear birds—finches, no doubt, and linnets—twittering in the apple-trees, which are planted very close together, after the French fashion, so that a kind of twilight reigns beneath. Yet the lengthening rays of the afternoon sun have found their way in here; they fall in rich golden pools of light upon the green grass.

I rest here. I am all alone. Down the middle of the orchard runs a long straight trench, unscathed, untouched. Around it in serried ranks lies a full battalion of infantry—asleep.

So close to the firing-line! Mystified, yet doubting, I creep round the trench towards the road.

A pool of golden sunshine falls direct upon one of the sleeping figures which lies rather apart, the face upturned, one arm extended—a typically Teuton face. The uniform is grey, the facings red, the belt and pouches and the boots black. The expression and attitude of the young man are peaceful and calm, if a little unnatural. Not a quiver, not a sound.

I glance at the other figures as I creep by. They, too, are very peaceful, very quiet, very happy. Nearly all are Englishmen and, looking at them, I realise that I am in the presence of a great fraternity of soldiers. Nothing shall disturb their rest again: neither shells, nor bullets, nor the call of duty.

In the sunny meadow beyond, a clergyman and two helpers have begun their work of burying the dead.

A dry ditch bordered these orchards where such

desperate fighting had taken place on the previous day. Lurking in this ditch I found two Scots Guard stretcher-bearers apparently none too keen to enter the fray. On the other side of it ran the by-road which led direct to the dressing-station. I was now very tired, and it seemed suitable that the two men should do their bit of work. Between the three of us we applied a couple of field dressings.

I could not have presented a very elegant appearance on this occasion—soaked to the skin with the brackish water of the foul ditches, clothes caked with mud and stained yellow up one side, and putties torn to shreds. Part of my equipment I had discarded at various points; the remainder was unrecognisable under layers of mud.

So presently my ten stone ten was hoisted up by the two stretcher-bearers and borne along the shell-stricken road. All this section to the dressing-station—about a quarter of a mile—had been the scene of heavy fighting the day before. It was a picture that in its stark reality appeared strange and awe-inspiring. Ammunition wagons, rushing up the road, had been caught by artillery fire and overturned or smashed. There they lay, half on the road, half off it. Dead horses blocked the ditch alongside, their legs protruding stiffly erect, their bodies half buried in mud and water, and all around a great litter of tackle and equipment.

The road itself was pitted and furrowed, and upon its surface were little drops and trails of blood where the wounded had been carried past. The milestones along this *via dolorosa* were the bodies of men who had fallen and died—some in the middle of the fairway and others just beside it, resting on the grass. In the fields and the orchards on either hand the attack had swayed to and fro, and these, too, were littered with relics. No attempt had been made to clear them away, for bullets still whistled past and shells screamed, though harmlessly, overhead.

I observed these things as I was borne along on the stretcher, the bearers of which laid it down in the road now and again to change hands or to rest. A constant procession of wounded passed by. Here and there detachments of troops or Red Cross men were awaiting orders by the roadside.

We came presently to the dressing-station—a ruined farm, whose bright red walls stood out stark and roofless. Here was a busy scene indeed. The place swarmed with activity, the air was alive with the purring sound of motors. Apart from the stream of wounded, on foot and on stretchers, constantly coming in—three-quarters of whom seemed to be hit in the head—doctors and Red Cross orderlies rushed to and fro, and in the open space where the by-road joined the main highway there stood groups of Staff officers, medical officers, motor-cyclist orderlies, and messengers. Two motor ambulances were ready to start off immediately, and in one of these my stretcher was placed.

It did not wait long. Three other stretchers were lifted in, one resting on the top tier beside my own, the others beneath us. The occupants of the ambulance are a sergeant, who moans restlessly, and a bucolic, bloodthirsty fellow, who loudly proclaims that he has been hit three times and has "done in" as many Germans. A slightly wounded comrade has accompanied him down to the ambulance, and now wishes him a safe journey home and a good holiday. Nor does this precious rascal cease to chatter volubly (to himself) as we rattle along, voicing his own peculiar opinion about the progress of the battle; and when the suffering sergeant presently tells him to "shut his row," the only retort is a volley of amiable blasphemy.

It is a ridiculous situation.

The fourth member of the party is a youthful subaltern in the Irish Rifles, who lies beside me, very still and quiet. His face is white as marble, his eyes are wide open; he seems to be half-conscious. Occasionally he moved his lips, and once clasps the roof-joist with his pallid hand, which presently falls limp across my chest. He does not move again, and when they lift him out he is dead.

The flap of the ambulance is left open, so that I am able to observe many things that happen on the rapidly receding road to the field hospital. There is great activity—Red Cross motors and big grey Staff cars rushing past, orderlies on bicycles and on horseback, Staff officers cantering along and numerous parties of soldiers on one mission or another. All the ruins of farmhouses by the roadside are occupied by troops.

We have not travelled far before we pass batches of German prisoners between armed guards, trudging stolidly along in file, their grey uniforms, little round caps, and unkempt faces suggesting a party of convicts. Weedy and uneven they are for the most part, and of no account compared with the fine men of the Prussian Guard whom I had seen prisoners just before I entered the battle.

Now we rattle through the streets of Estaires, whence a couple of days ago the Battalion had marched out at full strength. Then, leaving behind the noise of the market-place, we pass under an arch into a quiet courtyard. I ask the name of the place. It is a school for young priests. I glance once more at the composed face of him for whom there is to be no journey home, and am carried across the courtyard to a surgical room. Here a new dressing is applied, and at the same time I am inoculated against tetanus. My label for England is affixed, and I am taken to another room, a large, cool place, where two figures are already lying. One is a Scotch colonel, wounded in two places by shrapnel; the other, the same young doctor of the Scots Fusiliers whom I had found lying in the open that morning, having been shot while attending some of my own wounded.

An amiable attendant in a white suit immediately brings a cup of hot soup, relieves me of my pack and such equipment as remains on me, together with a good deal of mud, and produces a very welcome cigarette. Presently one of the priests appears—a grave man with an austere, sallow face, dressed in a rusty black cassock—and inquires of each whether he belongs to the Roman Catholic Church. Obtaining little satisfaction from anybody, he shuffles out, and we are left alone on our stretchers with our pains and our thoughts.

The curious silence of the place after the unspeakable din and confusion of the struggle round the mill is one of the strangest reactions imaginable. Not a sound but the occasional echo of a footstep down the cool stone passages comes to disturb our rest for many hours. Only the poor doctor moaned quietly to himself in his darkened corner.

Once an aeroplane sailed across the space of blue sky which could be seen through the open window, and its droning hum drifted in on the still air. Outside, there was a glimpse of a plane tree and a flower-garden, and a red brick wall, upon which, as afternoon passed into evening, the setting sun cast its lengthening shadows. I thought—by way of contrast—of the years and years of sunlit peace which must have lingered in this quiet place and of all the unsophisticated, retiring men who had learnt their lifelong lessons there.

Presently it was quite dark, and we were carried out one by one to the motor-ambulance, which travelled swiftly to the clearing hospital at Merville nine miles away.

It is five days since the battle, and after thirty-six hours at the field clearing hospital at Merville I was removed to Number Two Red Cross Hospital, Rouen, where I now am. Alas! my luck is dead out. It appears although I was labelled for England, I am not to be allowed home. The disappointment is the more galling because originally it was settled by the people here that I should return by the first convoy from Havre, and the doctor, who had strongly recommended it, told me so: I was only to stay a day or two. Then yesterday some new regulation came out, and a M.C. colonel came round and decreed that I should remain. I believe it is the same with a good many others. And if I had any influence here I could get home at once!

We are well looked after and I have a room to myself which is pleasant, also a very nice nurse and doctor, though otherwise one never sees a soul. I believe I have to undergo a very slight operation to-morrow, and am pretty sure I shan't be fit for the front for a month. I got the old bullet bang through the calf of my left leg; it missed the bone by a bare inch and drilled two neat holes, one on either side of my leg. It seems extraordinary that although chilled to the bone after struggling through streams and ditches chin-deep in poisonous water, still I suffer no after effects from my crawl. I consider myself very lucky to get off as cheaply as I have. I am afraid my company lost heavily, but Seymour, who got a shrapnel bullet through the head, is doing well, I learn. Warner too, when I last saw him, was all right. But Maurice Darby is killed. I know nothing about the rest who were behind us. We certainly had the hottest corner. It is rather difficult attempting to scribble in even a diary in bed, as I have to keep my leg straight, but it is so nice to be quiet again after all the noise and confusion.

To my great amusement, I see that the Paris *Daily Mail* have got me as a casualty with the following supplementary notice in a conspicuous position:—"Second Lieut. Ewart of the Scots Guards is among the list of casualties given out last night. The wounded officer is a son of Mr. Herbert and Lady Mary Ewart of 8, West Eaton Place, London, and is a cousin of the present Lord Arran." Rather droll!

It does seem hard to stay here when London is only twelve hours away.

Two days more have gone, and I am still here in Rouen and no nearer getting home. But I yet have hopes that I may do so. The doctor says he thinks he can manage it in a day or two, and I don't think he would raise my hopes without good reason. If I had had a dog's luck I should have been there by now.

I had my little operation done the day before yesterday. It hurt a bit afterwards, but I feel all right now except, of course, that I cannot move much. If only I was sure of going home, how happy I should be!

I see from the papers that poor Teddy Hulse was killed. I last saw him urging on his company as we left the trenches.

As the Head Surgeon seems determined upon it and

as I have been here a week, I really do think now they are going to send me home—it's over ten days since I was wounded. With luck I may go with the next convoy, but of course I cannot guess with the slightest certainty. It would be absurd if they did not, as I cannot be fit for hard work for a few weeks. My leg is decidedly groggy, though not painful, and my foot is crocked up owing mainly to marching on *pavé* roads. I do not look forward to loafing about here in Rouen, where there is nothing to do. These last few days have been very fine and sunny, and I have got out on to the verandah in a wheeled *chaise*, which was amusing. Here are to be found all the convalescent officers walking about and making conversation to the nurses. The triflings and badinage that go forward! Such jokes and sallies on the part of the young men—one never has heard! The only other alternative is Neuve Chapelle. With the older officers this is a sort of disease. The stories they tell are something shocking. They all try to cap each other with their yarns, until a poor devil is nowhere at all unless he has killed one hundred and fifty Germans with the butt-end of an entrenching-tool. One gets rather sick even of Neuve Chapelle.

I am beginning to wonder what has happened to my kit. I have absolutely nothing here except the uniform I was wearing when hit. My breeches had to be slit up the side and my tunic is a shocking sight, but I suppose it doesn't matter much. Only I hope I shall see my equipment and kit-sack again some day. I shall never see my pack (I relinquished that to fate at Estaires with my marked map), Burberry, or rug. In all probability this last is covering some mouldy old German at this moment.

And I—at this moment? Well, I shall enjoy a *good* dinner!

CHAPTER IV

CHRISTMAS 1915

I only hold disjunct impressions relating to my six months in England, impressions of days at Princess Beatrice's Hospital in Hill Street, at the Portals in Hampshire, at Broadleas, my cousin Margaret's house near Devizes, and of London and light service at Wellington Barracks. And here I am back in France again and my mind is focussed on realer things.

It is Tuesday, October 26th, 1915, and I have just got to Havre after quite a good journey. The sea was not rough, although there was a slight swell. It was an infinitely better journey than that memorable one of February. From what I can see I am not likely to stay here at Honfleur long before going up to the Second Battalion, for there is almost an over-congestion of officers and men. Nevertheless, the base camp is greatly improved since I was last here. I see a good deal of one, Fuller Maitland, who is a very pleasant fellow.

After having been here three days I am going up the line on the forty-eight-hour cattle-truck trip this evening to join the Battalion in rest billets—not with my own men, but in charge of Grenadiers and Irish Guards. I expect to be with the Battalion by Sunday morning. Except for leaving Fuller Maitland behind, I am not sorry. Honfleur soon proves itself to be a pretty rotten place to be at.

The weather has been quite fine since this morning, but yesterday was most unpleasant, although in the evening I went to Havre with several people in the Brigade to allay the misery. We dined at a strange sort of *café* and afterwards went to a music-hall, which was rather amusing but strangely different from Lena Ashwell's performance eight months ago. I'm off for a bath before starting.

In the last week I have had little to record. We are still in rest billets at Cantrainne with very little to do except go on an occasional route-march. I am keeping very fit, and the weather remains fine if rather cold. This morning there was a hard frost and brilliant sunshine.

We move off somewhere, I believe, three days hence (*i.e.* next Tuesday night, November 9th), and shall doubtless be in the trenches by the end of next week for a time. After that our programme is more or less uncertain, but it undoubtedly includes a lot of shifting about, and there are rumours of our going to a place a very long way from here—in fact, in a different part of the country. My Company Commander returned from leave to-day. He seems very decent—although different from Warner. His name is Arkwright, and he is a great hunting man—an M.F.H., I believe. A number of officers also arrived last night, some going up to the First Battalion, but I have heard nothing of Fuller Maitland. I don't know where he is or what he is doing, but I hope he comes to this Battalion soon. My servant from Wellington Barracks, Whorley, who left me at the base, since his old master wanted him, I have just replaced with an excellent fellow called Malcolm.

Knollys, who came out with me this time, has just arrived here from the Base. Alas! Fuller Maitland, he tells me, has gone away down the line with a digging battalion. As I suspected yesterday, we *are* moving from here on Tuesday, to a place about eight miles away, and will be in the trenches by the end of the week.

Thursday, November 11th. Four days since I last entered anything! I have been very busy. Our ten-mile march on Tuesday brought us to these billets which are about a mile from Merville (where I was after Neuve Chapelle) and we are close by the First Battalion. Our visit to the trenches is set for three days hence, for Sunday, and we are likely to be under fire for the next month or six weeks at least. I cannot say that I look forward to it, but I hope that the trenches are respectable. J. A. Stirling has succeeded Arkwright as my Company Commander, and at present we have a very strong Battalion, but I expect they will soon start going sick. Arkwright has gone home with a nervous breakdown. He was a nice chap and a good soldier.

My remark of a week ago about going sick seems to have been prophetic, for I am in the Casualty Clearing

Hospital, Merville, at the moment, having been taken queer on coming out after a brief spell in the trenches. I quite enjoyed myself there, having a heart-to-heart talk with the Germans. But on leaving felt very ill indeed. Now I feel better. I am not sure what the disease is, but the doctor says it may be jaundice. If not, I shall probably be back with the Battalion in a week or two.

I have been here in hospital for nearly a week, but go back to the Battalion five days hence on Wednesday, November 26th. I am feeling quite all right, but the doctor thinks I had better be on the safe side. It is certainly not exciting here, but nevertheless is preferable to the trenches. The weather is lovely, but very cold. People are constantly coming in and out. I have an Irish Guards officer with me, and yesterday I went out with him to luncheon in the local inn, which is reckoned a great dissipation.

From the crowded streets and from talk it seems that the whole Division is billeted around.

I have been meaning to record something ever since I rejoined the Battalion a week ago to-day, but somehow it has been *très difficile*. Yesterday, December 1st, I went over to a neighbouring town and had a good talk with an assembly of officers. There were a good many whom I knew there, including the Prince of Wales, who remembered me from Wellington Barracks. Before that there was a great battalion concert one night and a dinner-party. The Brigadier came and they had the Grenadiers' band. Several people got tight. It was a good concert. And now we are packing up to go into the trenches to-night for a twelve-day stay, which is not a very cheerful prospect, though the weather keeps fine and it is comparatively warm for December. It seems I must continue to *mean* to write.

We have just finished our twelve days in the trenches, thank God! and return to rest billets for six days to-morrow—a nine-mile march.

Our time has been very quiet so far as fighting went, though the Germans shelled us three or four times and our artillery continually strafed. Yesterday afternoon they put a 4-in. shell just behind my new dug-out and very nearly blew up the officers' kits which were lying there all packed up. I write *new* dug-out because about a week ago, a dug-out having fallen on some Welsh Guards, killing one and wounding three, the lot were condemned, among them my old one; and for a time I rested—for sleep was impossible—under a bit of corrugated iron in the fire-trench which I shared with a sergeant and a private. In fact, I have had a fairly hard time; what between Lonely Post, the trenches with their rats and mice worse than ever, and a five-hour patrol at night.

Lonely Post was a beastly place and a responsible one, as I was there all by myself. It was in a depressing part of the line on the borders of the battlefield of Neuve Chapelle. Some of the dead men of the Rifle Brigade still lay out in front, while behind, to cheer me up, there was a perfect forest of little mud graves and crosses, mostly very rough, and marked "In Memory of a British Soldier, R.I.P." In the distance I could see approximately the place where Seymour and I got wounded and poor Teddy Hulse was killed.

A night or two ago a party of the Fourth Grenadiers, who were next to us, made a raid on the German trenches. We were all on the *qui vive*, not knowing what might happen. Under cover of darkness they crept across No Man's Land, through the German wire, and up to the parapet. At a given time our guns opened fire and the Grenadiers rushed the German trench, scuppered the machine-gunners and spiked their gun. At the same time another lot ran along the German trench bombing every dug-out and bayoneting every German they met. On the blowing of a whistle they all jumped back over the parapet and raced back to our lines, having had one officer slightly wounded. It was a smart job. I watched from our parapet, and it was like a thing in a play, although of course I could not see all that was actually happening. The sky behind was lit up by the flashes of the guns, and presently there was a furious burst of rifle-fire from the German trenches, followed by the flash and boom of their guns from the Aubers Ridge and the flickering glare of innumerable star-lights and rockets which the Bosches sent up. Then all was dead still and dark, as if the curtain had been rung down.

I have never seen a better show in a small way. It lasted about a quarter of an hour, and a good many Germans must have been killed.

Last night, December 12th, we had some Welsh Fusiliers attached for instruction, and it was *très drôle* when they came into the trenches for the first time. They ducked and jumped about, apparently oblivious of the fact that there was a four-foot breastwork between them and the Germans.

To-day a Bosche aeroplane came over and it was shot at ineffectually. The whole affair rather reminded me of the London Zeppelin raids.

We are going back to the trenches to-night, December 20th, after a week in billets, and are rather busy putting things straight. We are going to be in the forts just behind the front line. I have had quite a nice time resting, with nothing much to do except read and go for long walks. I have just finished reading Compton Mackenzie's *Carnival* and am about to begin F. S. Oliver's *Ordeal by Battle*, which I will take with me. I wish there were more of Compton Mackenzie's books here.

It is difficult to realise that Christmas is but five days off.

Nothing exciting is happening except the usual strafing. I have just received an early Christmas parcel of food and a packet containing tobacco, pipes, chocolate, a pound cake, bedroom slippers, and a knitted scarf. I am going to distribute the smoking paraphernalia among the N.C.O.'s of my platoon.

I am writing from a fort about three-quarters of a

mile behind the front line. We go forward again to-morrow night. The trenches on Christmas Eve!

It is Christmas morning. As I gaze over the parapet on the drab landscape before me every feature, every rise or fall in the ground, every knoll, every hideous skeleton of shattered buildings, almost every tree, has its story, so consecrated for ever to the memory of the English race is the Aubers Ridge opposite—an inconsiderable, scarcely noticeable rise in the ground. So are the skeleton trees, the hedgerows and fields that fringe its summit, that climb its slope. So are the bright red and dark red roofs of buildings that cluster half-way up the slope and the tall factory chimney in their midst, that of Aubers itself. In the foreground is a village absolutely shattered. It is scarcely possible to see the brown roofs, the stark walls, and vari-coloured ruins, amid the trees. Then comes the church—a ghostly shell, dominating the flat scene. And behind the trenches is a row of tall elms and poplars, looking monstrous in the mist, these marking the line of a road. Immediately in front of them is a big farmstead with a courtyard and a square little home-field—an untidy heap of red bricks amid four naked walls.

Between the irregular lines of the trenches, with their jumbled white sandbags and untidy earth parapets, is a stream marked by a line of twisted brown willows bent to every conceivable grotesque shape. The stream runs down the middle of No Man's Land, which is itself a place of coarse grasses hiding little mouldering heaps of grey and khaki—the slain of Festubert, of Neuve Chapelle and late September (heaps of old clothes or fallen scarecrows, they look like), of knobs and unexpected pits, of earthy holes and water-logged ditches. And here our men meet the Germans.

So soon as it grows light this morning, we start peeping at each other over the top of the parapet . . . calling across to each other. And presently, at about 7.50, a German stands up openly on the parapet and waves his arms. He is followed by two in field-grey overcoats and pill-box caps. Then they come out all down the line, stand up on the parapet, wave, shout, and finally swarm forth from their trenches on either side.

A British sergeant is shot dead almost at the outset, as he stands on the parapet. But this makes no difference. It must be an accident. The supreme craving of humanity, the irresistible, spontaneous impulse born of a common faith and a common fear, fully triumph.

And so the grey and khaki figures surge towards each other as one man. The movement has started on the right. It spreads like contagion. Only we officers, the sentries, and a few non-commissioned officers remain in our trench. The men meet at the willow-lined stream; they even cross it and mingle together in a haphazard throng. They talk and gesticulate, and shake hands over and over again. They pat each other on the shoulder and laugh like schoolboys, and leap across the little stream for fun. And when an Englishman falls in and a Bosche helps him out there is a shout of laughter that echoes back to the trenches. The

Germans exchange cigars and pieces of sausages, and *sauerkraut* and concentrated coffee for cigarettes, and bully-beef and ration-biscuits and tobacco. They express mutual admiration by pointing and signs. It is our leather waistcoats and trench-coats that attract their attention; it is their trench-overalls, made of coarse canvas, that attract ours. We shout "Hullo, Fritz!" "Good morning, Fritz!" "Merry Christmas!" "Happy Christmas!" "How's your father" "Come over and call!" "Come and have breakfast," and the like, amid roars of laughter. Even confidences are exchanged in broken English.

"When's the war going to end?"

"After the Spring offensive."

"Yes—after the Spring offensive."

"What sort of trenches have you?"

"Rotten! Knee deep in mud and water. Not fit for pigs."

"Aren't you sick of the war? We are!"

"Not a bit."

And the information is even vouchsafed that our Christmas Eve bombardment had caused the Germans a lot of casualties.

So for ten brief—all too brief—minutes there is peace and goodwill among the trenches on Christmas Day.

Then from the trenches of the Ninety-fifth Bavarian Reserve Infantry Regiment two officers in black accoutrements and shiny field-boots come out, wishing to take photographs of our Tommies, and offering them cigars. Their request is refused, and presently they say:

"You will have five minutes to get back to your trenches before our artillery will open fire."

And it does. And two or three men are wounded almost at once. But for twenty-four hours not a shot is fired on either side. A common brotherhood of suffering—or is it an act of God, or just human curiosity?—has united Englishman and Bavarian in fraternity on the battlefield this grey Christmas morning which no one on either side who has taken part in this quaint scene will ever forget.

CHAPTER V

INTO THE SALIENT

It is January 1st, 1916, and for winter the weather is extraordinarily mild and agreeable. We celebrated the New Year last night in a simple way. Stirling went out to dinner, but Knollys and I had a Grenadier and a stray artillery officer in for a meal. The servants and orderlies made a sing-song and we made some whiskey punch.

To-morrow night the men are going to have a great New Year's dinner in rest billets in Merville, and so are some officers with, I believe, a lot of generals—the "blokes," as the men call them. The Germans have livened up here lately and have shelled us mildly several times without doing any damage. My company has been garrisoning the forts just behind the line—a rotten job, as we don't get to our reserve billets when the others do. As for companionship, we are reduced to only three officers.

One piece of important intelligence gleaned is that we are really moving off down South very soon—in fact, it is definitely settled, although the exact date is not fixed. We are following Lord Cavan to his new command. I fear that my leave is farther off than ever, since, owing to the fraternisation incident a week ago, all leave in the regiment is stopped indefinitely. It is rotten luck, as I am qualified for it and in fact am, I believe, next subaltern on the list. I fear, too, that when leave is resumed all the senior officers will make a dash for it. However, I must hope for the best.

Various Army Battalions of Kitchener's have been attached to us lately for instruction, and the extra work they make is a bit of a nuisance. They belong to the newly-arrived Welsh Division.

I see a good deal of the Prince of Wales in this sector. He joined Stirling and myself on the march the other day, riding a bicycle, and he often dines at Headquarters.

I hope we shall have only one more turn of twelve days in trenches before coming out for a long rest.

Three weeks and more since I last entered anything! Well, a brief spell of English leave has intervened. Now I am back again with the Battalion after my journey. I stayed one night at Boulogne at a rotten hotel and left after luncheon the next day. I had quite a comfortable journey up the line with the Welsh Guards' Quartermaster, and he lent me a horse on which I rode out, and I stayed the night with him. I walked down to the trenches at cockcrow the next morning. Stirling was there when I arrived, but Knollys had just left on his leave.

I only had to spend one night in the trenches before we came into reserve billets here last night. The Germans are much more active. Yesterday they put a big shell into one of the forts and we had three men killed and ten wounded. A few minutes ago they put six big shells into the middle of the village here, and if I can judge by the excitement outside, they seem to have done a lot of damage.

To-morrow we march back for six days' rest. The great move has now been put off a month and we are going back to the trenches, which is rather sickening, as the idea has always been that we were to rest after January 26th, and that eagerly awaited date is now only two days ahead.

In the last fortnight a good deal has happened. I am now with the Seventh (Guards) Entrenching Battalion down on the Somme, and we are stationed in a camp in a wood. I came straight out of the trenches and along the line in a luggage van and also on a motor-lorry. This place is well within shelling range, and the Germans seem to do a good bit of bombarding, but they never actually put any shells in here, and I feel a lot safer than at our last Reserve billets. However, it is a good deal less comfortable, as we live under canvas with no sort of firing or way of getting hot water.

This Battalion is a composite one of Grenadiers, Scots Guards, Coldstream, Irish, and Welsh. There are about six Scots Guards officers, but ones I hardly know, mostly quite late-joined. The work consists of repairing the trenches and digging a new line just behind. It is not very interesting, but then we don't overwork!

The Second Battalion, I hear, is just going away back for a month's rest and after that, I believe, they go

North to Ypres, but not to the Salient. It is hard to tell, for the most extraordinary rumours seem to get about. Recently the Division has not been in action at all.

The weather all the week since Sunday, when I last entered anything, has been simply foul—bitter cold wind and sheets of rain coupled with oceans of mud. Living in tents it has been frightful. Even the officers' mess here consists of a wooden hut. However, I like this place all right, as the men here are a very decent lot and the atmosphere is pleasant.

I have a company of my own—two hundred and twenty men—and they are all Scots Guards. I have also four very nice subalterns.

The Germans shell the roads all round, but miss the camp, not suspecting this wood.

The life is not a bad one, although I anticipate it will become rather monotonous after a time. I wish I could expect leave soon, but at the earliest I could not get any for two months yet.

I have been ill and in hospital. It seems my pleasant life here is not destined to continue, as I am to be recalled to the Second Battalion, since they want a full complement when going North to Ypres. However, the C.O. and the doctor are dead against my going to them for at least a fortnight.

Work is very hard here now, and this morning I

paraded with the Company shortly after seven o'clock, and trekked seven miles in wagons to the Reserve Line, worked on a light railway until four in the afternoon, and did not get back to the camp until nearly five. I am now the only Scots Guards officer here.

The weather fortunately since my return from hospital has much improved, and this camp is pretty now in the Spring. Nightingales abound and sing at night.

I am to report to the Guards Division five days hence, on Monday next, May 15th, and I depart from here the day before. I have had a little leave since going sick, and in the interim a great deal seems to have happened. My Company has been in and out of the line now for two months. They went in to the south of the Potijze Road on the evening of March 16th, and on April 19th were in their first serious engagement. Yesterday, May 9th, Brigadier (Heyworth) got sniped, and we are due at his funeral at Brandhoek.

In some ways I shall be sorry to leave here; in others not. The country is very pleasant, but the hours of work are very, very long and terribly monotonous. The Bosche keeps quiet, but on our side there is evidently something impending before long. The weather has been rotten, but is now better, though still cold.

I have only been here resting with the Second Battalion (who had just come out of the trenches) four days, but that has been quite long enough to see what sort of a place this is. The first night the Bosches made an aeroplane raid and dropped bombs all round the camp. The second night they repeated the performance. The third night there was a gas alarm from the front line and we all stood to arms. Shelling all day and Bosche aeroplanes constantly over; ours have no chance. At the present moment the Germans are shelling heavily a road about three hundred yards away.

This camp is in the middle of a beautiful wood and the weather is lovely and one can sit out of doors and read.

To-night, May 19th, we go into the Salient for a week to work. The Division is really coming out altogether for a month, but one Battalion in each Brigade has got to do an extra week's work, and by bad luck this takes us. Stirling will be commanding our Company, and Knollys will be with us. The country here is much prettier than I expected from what I heard of it on the Somme, but I believe that Ypres itself and the Salient are unholy Hell, especially in the last few days since the Division marched out here.

When this slow summer dusk begins to deepen, we can begin to stir in the trenches. We have been here now nearly a week, and the procedure is always the same. All day long the men have slept or dozed in the warm sunshine, lain in their dug-outs—little holes in the parados—or nodded on the fire-step in a sultry atmosphere of buzzing bluebottles and occasional shots from snipers' rifles. For here one cannot move or walk about by day, the sniping (from dominating positions) is too keen. But when the dusk deepens into that pearly-blue light which for a man moving is the most invisible, long files of men start off to join us and the sound of tramping feet is heard on the roads.

Night by night—and all night long—those files of ghostly figures move along the roads towards us. Ration-parties, carrying-parties, parties with working material, engineers, generals and officers of inspection rank, parties with pick and shovel, and many other sorts of workers move along these roads. A little later, and we see them, patiently bending under their loads, silhouetted against the rising moon. Some of the carriers are so strangely silent they seem like ghosts of men tramping across the plain, only their feet go pit-patter, pit-patter, when they are quite near; these are wearing long thigh-boots with rubber soles.

And they have to hurry. For the midsummer night is short, and between the grey twilight and the rosy dawn there is but a space of four hours. God help him who is caught by the sunshine in an open place!

And with the deepening dusk a new life begins with us in the trenches. The buzz of bluebottles and the crack of the sniper's rifle give place to the chatter of machine-guns and the slow glare of the star-lights. Shadow and mystery creep in where was the stark nakedness of shell-holes, broken trees, and lines of battered sandbags.

To take one instance of this life, that of my working-party. Slowly, with many exclamations, pauses, and much hard swearing, it now moves along the crowded trench, then out into the sap. There is a little narrow ridge between the parapet of the sap and a chain of enormous shell-holes. In these the water glistens. The men are silent now that they are out in the middle of No Man's Land scarcely seventy yards from the German trench. Only when one of them trips over the frequent loose strands of wire or stumbles into a shell-hole do I hear a scuffle, followed by a muttered curse.

It is a question of digging a new trench. Get them lined out quickly, quietly, three yards apart; let each man work his hardest to dig himself in. They know it too, and put their backs into the task. It is surprising how quickly they get into the ground considering the heavy, spongy state of all this water-logged country. Quickly they throw up the earth in front, which gives a feeling of protection, even if a somewhat illusory one. Nor can the task be considered in any way pleasant. A peculiar and horrible stench clings to the ground, thicker and more fœtid in some places than in others, but all-pervading. It is the sickly stench of dead bodies. Strange and sometimes fearsome things are dug out of the ground. All drab and muddy, yielding and soft, so that you could not recognise it as a human thing was the body of a German. There was no head, only the trunk. Someone cuts off two of his buttons as a memento, another finds his rifle, completely rusted and caked in mud. Then they dig up a machine-gun, rusted too, and mud-caked, which must have been buried in the last battle. The curious thing about this is that it is evidently a British gun converted by the Germans, for the lock is German, so is the barrel. Once cleaned it will be serviceable again and will be re-converted to fire British ammunition.

The night is a fairly quiet one. Yet apart from the stertorous breathing of the men labouring at their trench, the darkness is full of sounds. Now it is the dismal wail of a stray bullet hungrily seeking a billet. Now it is the clack-clack-clack of the machine-guns chattering to each other, like demons in Hell. One of these sweeps round—traverses, the gunners call it—regularly every few minutes, and the terrifying rush of the bullets causes every man to lie flat on his stomach. A machine-gun, when traversing, nearly always sweeps back again, so it is not safe to get up at once. Every now and then a succession of explosions, sharp, yet heavy and dull, unlike that of a shell, proclaims that bombs are being thrown not far off—probably from adjacent saps. Occasionally through the night a terrific explosion causes the atmosphere to reverberate and everyone to start. It is a minenwerfer bomb bursting somewhere away on the right, and it is followed by a succession of sharp reports and heavy explosions from one of our own trench-guns retaliating. In the silent pauses between these sounds may be heard the harsh cry of some bird—I know not its name—which haunts the coarse grass and secret places of the Salient. Occasionally a distant rattle and a harsh grating sound become audible—the German transport on the roads beyond the ridge. A lighter and more continuous grating sound is made by the trolleys rolling along one of the numerous light railways which run just behind the enemy's front line. Every now and again, too, in silent pauses, the barking of dogs may be distinguished —these are the German pets which they keep in their trenches.

Two or three times in the night the whole horizon is of a sudden lit up by the vivid flashes of our own guns, so vivid that one may distinguish trees and other objects against their background; then one hears a distant rumble followed by the roar of the shells, and observes the quick glare as they burst on the enemies' second line.

Strange figures come prowling through the darkness —one cannot tell for certain whether friend or foe. Ever and anon the star-lights go up, and in their cold radiance one may see those figures standing still as statues. Yet they would be better advised to throw themselves down. They are the covering-parties and the engineers moving out in front. Once the man who fires the Verey pistol can be plainly seen, and then one knows that the Germans, too, are out in No Man's Land. Once three lights go up in quick succession, and simultaneously two shots ring out. These are followed immediately by a loud outcry close at hand, which shows that at least one of the bullets has done its work —"Oh! oh! oh!" Gradually the loud cries sink into a pitiful murmur as a child in pain, and presently this lapses into silence. "Pass the word down for the stretcher-bearer!" They lay him down in a shell-hole —it is an officer of engineers, shot through both thighs. They do not think he is bad, but the moon shines down upon a face unnaturally still and pallid, and when the doctor comes he is dead.

A fresh feeling in the air and a faint lightening in the sky beyond the German lines suggest that daybreak is not far off. The men have dug their trench, many are resting on their spades, perspiring profusely. They prepare to move off. Suddenly a machine-gun opens and one of them sits down quickly, clasping his ankle with both hands. "Oo-er," he mutters, "I'm hit. It don't 'arf hurt." A comrade takes off his puttees and unlaces his boot. "Is it a Blighty one, d'ye think?" inquires this victim anxiously, and upon being told that it probably is, since he has been shot through the ankle, he becomes quite cheerful despite the pain.

Soon the word is passed down to lead back, and so the men file once more along the sap into the main trench. From the woods afar off comes the call of a cuckoo, and gradually the various points of the landscape appear. Everybody makes tea, and before long is enjoying a hearty breakfast, followed by a long sleep.

That last week in the Salient was an awful strain, and I am glad to be out resting in camp again. We are having quite a good time, but really it is not much of a rest, as Roger Tempest, our Battalion Commander, who has recently returned from leave, works everybody devilish hard, and this morning there was a ten-mile route march. Also we are constantly on the move. We go into billets to-morrow, May 28th, for a short time, then nearer the line, then back again here for about ten days and go back to the Salient about June 10th, and I am afraid we have the worst part of it this time.

This is a pleasant wooded country. While I was on fatigue the other day in a wood—I had Hardy's *Far from the Madding Crowd* with me—the G.S.O. drove up with the Prince of Wales. I was surprised, as I thought he was (metaphorically) on the other side of the world. I had a long talk with them, and the Prince, looking very sunburnt, was very affable and asked numerous questions.

There are rumours of peace in the air, but I can't say I believe them. I hear a farm where we billeted recently was shelled to pieces yesterday. So that's luck!

I went around Ypres the other day—the Germans were shelling all the time I was there—and saw all the sights of the town, and some very strange things, including two 17-cm. shell-holes. The whole place is razed to the ground, not a house standing except the prison, but some of the neglected, overgrown gardens are very pretty.

We have had lovely summer weather; burning hot days and cool nights. I enter this in at a farmhouse where we have been billeted some four days, about nine miles back from the line—a very peaceful spot indeed, and I am sorry we are going to move off to camp to-morrow, June 1st, with a prospect of a hot eight-mile march.

Yesterday evening I made a very pleasant bicycling expedition with Knollys to a very picturesque town which stands on a hill in the middle of a plain and is one of the oldest towns in Flanders. We started after tea, and got there for an excellent dinner, which we ate on the verandah of the hotel overlooking the plain. Some of the country around is really very delightful, and there are a few handsome châteaux hidden among the woods.

As the front line is said to be a very bad place just now, nobody is looking forward to going back.

I am writing this in some very good billets at Wormhoudt, a good way back and even out of sound of the guns. We had the hell of a march back the day before yesterday, June 8th, fifteen miles. It seems we do not go into the front line to-day, as was expected—in fact, not until the 15th.

The regimental band has come out from London under Minto, who is attached to us, and we also had the bagpipes, which played alternately all the way. They bucked the French people by playing the *Marseillaise* and other patriotic airs going through the towns, and the First Grenadiers with their band came behind. So it was a great show.

Leave has now been reduced to five days in the Second Army, which is a pretty bad business; it takes me, however, for a spell about June 30th.

There has been a lot of fighting going on up here, and is likely to be more by all accounts. We stood to arms two days and two nights, expecting to make a counter-attack for the Canadians, but were not required. Work is still very hard under Roger Tempest.

It is the 17th of June and we are not yet in the line, but we marched fourteen miles yesterday, the first stage up towards it, and to-morrow we go into Brigade Reserve, which means another six- or seven-mile march. As far as I can see, it will be at least three weeks before we get our eight days' promised rest. The line, from all accounts, is very bad, and at one point only forty yards from the Bosches, who strafe both day and night.

The guns went all last night, to the northward, also the gas sirens. It was one of the heaviest bombardments I have ever heard. We stood to arms in the middle of the night and were actually ordered to move, but a few minutes later the counter-order came. The Germans attacked with gas, but we have heard no details. Altogether the atmosphere is electric, and anything may happen from moment to moment: it is only a question of waiting. I only hope again for the luck of a Blighty wound that I had in March 1915. As for my leave, which is due in less than a fortnight now, owing to the above circumstances, I have very little hope of getting it, I learn, and it would be only five days in any case.

If anything happens to Stirling, I am to be in command of the Company, since I am the senior subaltern in the Battalion, and, I believe, senior in the regiment. It seems strange with only twenty-two months of service.

With a dose of the line impending, I wish I could get some morphine tablets.

We have been here on the outskirts of Ypres for three days, since June 18th, and now, at the hour when rightly I must start out with an engineer on our evening's tramp, our dug-out looks curiously seductive and homelike. There lie the remains of a late supper; there are the two beds and the two sets of pyjamas; there is the book left open at the page half-read; and there are the gramophone records lying in an untidy heap beside the gramophone. The atmosphere is pungent with tobacco smoke, but warm and comfortable. The servants are just going to sleep. Darkness has long since fallen.

Outside the mist creeps in, creeps out, and round about. Like a ghost, like a wraith, it steals along the dim streets whose secrets are buried beneath tons of bricks and masonry, beneath heaps and heaps of ruins. At first I can see nothing in the filmy darkness after the brilliance of the dug-out; instinct alone guides my footsteps. In the dug-out all sound was deadened; one could hear nothing from without. But now I discover that the guns are firing in Ypres itself—fitfully yet frequently their banging and booming awake a thousand echoes. Every time a gun fires, the reflection of the flash lights up jagged ruins, a naked wall, or the skeletons of houses. It is evidently the beginning of a slow bombardment.

Across a desert open space we pick a way, then

stumble over blocks of fallen masonry and balks of timber in the lee of a walled garden. One feels that tom-cats ought to be yowling and spitting on the top of the wall; but even the tom-cats have fled. Silence, moist, heavy, mysterious, settles everywhere between the reports of the guns. At the city gate there are a wakeful sentry and a wakeful sergeant who says "Good-night" in a hearty voice. In the recesses of a kind of cave which does duty as a gate-house he has a noble fire burning, around which I can just distinguish the prostrate forms of his comrades peacefully slumbering. The sentry opens a door and we are outside the lines plonk-plonking across a plank bridge. There is water underneath—I can feel rather than see it—water that lies black and stagnant and seems to listen.

Out in the grass familiar sounds come to the ears. It is only a mile and a half to the trenches, and the machine-guns are chattering busily. No sooner does the Bosche start a steady burst of conversation than a couple of Lewis guns respond with demoniacal laughter. Farther away another Bosche joins in angrily, while the sniper's rifle interjects sharp occasional comments. Thus at times the dusk is full of sounds. Strangely, and for a moment, Verey-lights can be seen above the mists, quickly to vanish; the far-stretching panorama of the front outlined by star-shells is hidden to-night. Southward the great cannon roll in a dim unceasing chorus; near at hand the batteries in Ypres fire at irregular intervals, and the shells, whistling overhead, burst with a quick glare and crash along the German front line. Bombs are exploding, too. Deep, sullen detonations, three or four at a time, shake the earth and make the darkness tremble.

For us, the night never loses its fears. They creep up with the mists which wreathe and sidle round, now dense, now lifting thinly; they belong to the hideous unknown things which lurk on old battlefields. A sinking moon strives to penetrate the mist, and sometimes it succeeds, so that all the world becomes silvery and opaque. Away to the left I can just distinguish in this delicate gloom the dusky outlines of what has been a noble convent—a girls' school. But I cannot discern more than a very few yards of the ground ahead. It is pock-marked with innumerable shell-holes, and we frequently stumble and lurch forward into the long, rank thistles and nettles. Sometimes we cross a narrow weed-grown path that once has been a main road; sometimes we have to leap an old gun-pit or disused grass-fringed communication trench; sometimes a landmark is missed; and sometimes, when the fog grows dense, we seem to come to a dead end. Then my engineer companion, who knows every pathway, almost every shell-hole, pauses and takes his bearings, partly by the star-lights, partly by the bursting shells on the German front line. A mile behind, a broken city sleeps as one sleeps who can suffer no more.

Climbing a sandbag breastwork, we come to a stretch of hard road bordered at first by twisted willows which convey the fancy of fir trees in an upland country. This road runs straight into the front-line trench and on into the German lines; swept by more than one machine-gun, it is the most dangerous part of the whole journey. We waste no time, but hustle along, bending low, for every now and then a moonbeam succeeds in piercing the mist and silhouettes our figures far above the level of the trenches. The engineer has run this gauntlet, often alone, night after night, for close upon two years. Then we jump down into the trench, which is obviously new and clean and handsomely floored with duck-boards. The mist has momentarily dispersed and the new sandbags gleam white, washed by the moonshine. At present there is no parados. It was close by here that in the warm haze of a still June morning a short time ago there opened a bombardment as brief and terrible as any even this war has seen. It lasted only four hours, but those holding the front line were wiped out almost to a man. Then the grey Wurtembergers swarmed over at a leisurely walk, and now the château immediately opposite is a couple of hundred yards behind the German lines.

We have not passed more than two of the neatly-made traverses before the rich accents of the Far West are borne to our ears. There they are, a party of "Canucks," working quite unconcernedly outside their trench, putting the finishing touches to an artistic piece of sandbagging. An officer is superintending, and having passed the time of night with him, we hurry on to where a dug-out is being hollowed from the bowels of the earth. To reach this point the quicker, my engineer friend—who by long familiarity with the place has grown venturesome—announces his intention of taking a short cut across No Man's Land. The mist has fallen again, but no sooner are we out in a waste of shell-holes half-filled with water and much encumbered with loose strands of barbed wire than it lifts like a curtain and the moon peeps out as light as day. Almost simultaneously a German machine-gun opens very close and the bullets seem to sizzle over our backs. A sniper fires four or five shots in quick succession and, half standing, half crouching, as we are on the top of the ground barely two hundred yards from the Germans, we fancy we are spotted. Probably, as a matter of fact, we are not; but probabilities seem doubtful quantities out in the middle of No Man's Land in bright moonlight. So we sink down flush with the ground and lie there breathlessly for many minutes. Shall we be seen when we rise again? I breathe hard and think of home! Then the machine-gun traverses once more with a hurricane rush of bullets, and head to heel we hug the ground yet closer. Bombs are bursting with terrific reverberation not far away—whether hostile or otherwise it is impossible to say—while a retaliating Stokes gun produces a series of shattering explosions. The wail of shells overhead, though British, and their quick flash and burst on the German front line, shake the nerves as much as anything. Most dangers are rather imaginary than real: even more common is it to be not quite sure whether one is in danger at all!

Taking the earliest opportunity to double across No Man's Land to the nearest trench, we arrive eventually at the entrance to the first experimental deep dug-out. And what a feeling of security it gives to descend the very steep, greasy stairs, down, down, down into the bowls of the earth! Not even a "Minnie" could touch one here. What a moist and clammy heat! Everything is reeking damp. The floor and sides of this completed portion are of wood and very moist. Wavering candles provide the necessary light. In a side chamber opening from the main gallery the off-shift are asleep on eight wire-netting beds arranged like bunks on board ship. Snoring they are, manfully, and also in a similar gallery farther on. Then the woodwork stops, and I come upon the working shift stripped to the waist, sweating away at the earthy wall with pick and shovel or removing the bluish soil in wheelbarrows to the shaft, whence it is hauled up and used for parapet-making. Welsh miners they are, these great damp, hairy, brawny fellows, literally dripping perspiration, and the sergeant in charge—or foreman, as he prefers to call himself—speaks a queer North Country lingo that recalls the first time one went down a coal-mine. Night and day in the warm semi-darkness the gang is working, and so for three days, when they return to the ramparts for a rest or go right back to billets for a week.

After three-quarters of an hour's deep technical discussion and inspection it is time to start back, and once more we find ourselves breathing the night air, which now seems chilly. Close at hand a sentry is humming to himself some queer ditty of the Western world. Voices can be heard gaily chattering where an invisible group is at work building a new dug-out. Farther away a long chain of figures, each carrying a burden, can just be perceived gliding phantom-like through the mist. It is a carrying-party tramping home along the road. Life stirs on every hand—life, swarming, workaday, unconcerned. Ant-like activity seethes under the cloak of night. An hour hence the early sunbeams will discover nothing more human than empty trenches, shell-holes, and stinks.

Striking across country, we hurry back before daylight shall make that part of the front a death-trap. The first quarter of an hour or so, when stray bullets zip past the ears or hum drearily, is nervous work. After that we pick our way carefully and in a leisurely fashion among the thistles and the shell-holes. It is with a feeling of indescribable satisfaction—as of a good night's work done and a long day's rest earned—that we cross the wooden bridge again and enter the ramparts. I am conscious, too, of a keen appetite for breakfast. Morning is at hand, and soon the grey daylight will be stealing in among the streets and ruins of the stricken city. How beautiful it will look then! Summer in Flanders, I feel certain, holds a record for wonderful dawns and sorrowful dreams.

Outside the entrance to the dug-out we linger meditatively to smoke a cigarette in the first freshness of the coming day. Sparrows are twittering volubly in a score of shy gardens that, riotous with greenery, hide like tear-drops amid the desolate houses. Pigeons that once were fed by hand in the Grande Place now croon from stony pinnacles, surveying their fallen world. On the opposite wall the legend "Chocolat Menier, Dunkerque," confronts me with the message of bygone civilisation. There is a roseate flush in the sky above the ramparts, the morning star is jewelled in a setting of palest gold and hard turquoise-blue.

We move up into the front line to-night, June 22nd, leaving our snug and safe dug-outs along the banks of the Canal.

A number of aeroplanes are strafing to-day, and one of ours was shot down close here. We walked up to look at it soon afterwards: it was smashed to pieces and the pilot killed, shot through the face. Last night and this morning five of our aeroplanes went overhead and raided the Bosches. Things are a bit quieter here, but they were very agitated last week and earlier on in this, when big things were supposed to be imminent, and may be still for aught I know.

We had the Prince of Wales to luncheon on Sunday, and he was very cheerful. They let him go up to the front line afterwards.

I have had a pretty lively time here in the front line during the last ten days. A chap with me got knocked clean over by concussion from a minnenwerfer bomb which killed four men, so he has gone down to G.H.Q. on a course.

We are waiting for further news from the South. So far what we have heard is good, as we seem to have done the first job on the Somme all right. The troops next to us made a very successful raid the other night, which was preceded by a terrific half-hour's bombardment. Soon we are due in a rest camp, thank God.

We are kept pretty busy even when out in reserve. We have had seven more or less quiet days in camp, though the Bosches started heavily shelling the only available town, which had to be evacuated, so we didn't stay there long.

I went out riding a good deal, but the country hereabouts is not very interesting. Last night, July 14th, we came down into the Brigade Reserve and go into the front line on Tuesday night, July 17th. We are next door to the French this time, being the extreme left-hand company of the whole British line; there is just the Canal between us. I believe it is much quieter than the lines we have been in. By all accounts, the French spend most of their time sketching and shouting remarks across to the Bosches.

Things still seem to be going very well down South, and our people were evidently very near using cavalry the other day. I hear Haig has sacked several Generals. I also hear from official sources that, although the Bosches have never taken a man away from here, they have now only two Divisions (one at Verdun and one farther South in reserve) on the whole Western Front, and three in reserve on the Eastern Front, also one at Constantinople. So that is encouraging.

Lord Cavan made a speech to the Fourth Grenadiers the other night, from which they deduce that the Allies are going to be in no hurry to win the war, but will let things take their course for another twelve months, by which time, military opinion says, the Bosches will be in a bad way. For my part I greatly doubt whether Haig will try to push on much farther than he is now, as he has all the best of the ground for the Winter. I do not believe we shall make a serious attempt to break through till next Spring. Judging from this and other sources, one would gather that the earliest anticipated termination of the war is seventeen months hence, December 1917.

Stirling has been away for a few days, so I have had command of the Company. We were inspected by the new Brigadier (C. E. Corkran) on Wednesday, who expressed himself as very pleased on the whole.

All the pipers have gone to a big Allied review in Paris.

Still in Brigade Reserve we are lazing through this dreamy, hot afternoon of July 17th among the leafy surroundings of the Château Trois Tours, about a couple of miles behind the front line. Some sleep, some bathe in the artificial lake; and some read books or write letters, half lying, half sitting in the shade of the trees. It is a modern château such as the *bourgeois* love, turreted, jerry-built, and doll's-house like, but luxurious withal in its greenery and silence.

Save for the constant buzzing of aeroplanes overhead, few sounds are borne on the light westerly breeze which blows towards the trenches. But all afternoon reports keep coming in from the front line; the trenches are being pounded to nothing, nobody quite knows what to expect. Last night there was a raid, and now the Bosches are retaliating. To-night there is to be a relief. None look forward to it, and the ceaseless roo-coo-roo-coo-coo of the wood-pigeons in their leafy fastnesses makes one long for the infinite peace of an English summer.

The evening comes, and an hour before dusk the men parade for the trenches in the grass-grown farm-yard. By small parties, a platoon at a time, they march away, some to follow cross-country tracks towards the Canal, others going by the direct road. It is a calm and lovely aftermath, the sun setting in a golden haze, blue mists creeping up all around; the heat of the day is succeeded by a delightful freshness. Nevertheless clouds of dust rise from the road, for, as dusk falls, the great evening tide of traffic sets towards the trenches. Ration-parties, relieving-parties, fatigue-parties, all moving in file; motor-lorries, ambulances, motor-cyclists, officers on horseback, orderlies on bicycles, quartermasters and quartermaster-sergeants driving mess-carts—all form part of a steady stream that flows through the first battered village. At the cross-roads the main stream ceases, the reliefs turn to the left, heading straight for the Canal bank, and once more I can hear the pit-a-patter, pit-a-patter of trench boots. Queer Chinese figures the men look in their round tin-hats, heavy-laden with kit as they are, the rifle slung on the shoulder.

Now the nervous work begins, for often at this hour of the relief the road is sprayed with shrapnel. Every-body much prefers to travel by the grass tracks, but there is not room for all. However, the twilight is still and breathless, not a sound but the distant rattle of traffic and the pit-a-patter of the men's feet on the road. An occasional star-light rising and falling in the direction of the trenches, a low rumble far to the southward, and a passing flicker on the horizon which might be the reflection of German guns firing beyond the ridge or merely the playing of summer lightning, are almost the only signs of war. Presently we pass the stark shell of a ruined house, guardian of a rusty railway-line, overgrown with vegetation, and then come to the engineers' dump, where all traffic ceases. A congestion of troops in single file is waiting to cross the bridges. One seems to hesitate here on the threshold of Fate.

A Bosche machine-gun is trained on the wooden bridge which thirty or forty yards ahead spans the Canal. It may sweep round at any moment, but so accustomed are the men to travelling this way that they do not increase their pace by a hair's breadth. Rather are they inclined to pause in wonderment at the most weird and wonderful picture: the Canal by night.

Does it remind one most of a quiet backwater in Venice, or of a scene from the Earl's Court Exhibition, or of the imagined Styx where Charon ever ferries people from shore to shore; this waterway with its countless little lights blinking against high mysterious banks and its sullen, stagnant, lapping water which reflects the lights, the stars, and, sailing above, the cold moon? It looks seductive, exotic, populous, compared to the bleak, perilous world outside. The high banks are honeycombed, with dug-outs. All around is the busy human hum, shuffling, scuffling, mysterious.

The Canal is the clear-cut border-line between humanity and the shadowy nether-world of Ypres. Now the clack-clack-clack of the machine-guns is heard, a stray bullet or two whistles high over the road, and the star-lights seem much closer. An occasional rifle-shot punctures intervening silences. It is night, and with night in the Salient there comes a sense of loneliness and neighbouring death.

All scenes close behind the trenches are much the same, and this one is as others—void, barren, desolate. It is possible to travel all the way to the front line by communication-trench, but perversely the men prefer to walk as far as they are allowed to along the road. Well, the road is quicker even if a stray bullet or two does come that way. But beyond trench-headquarters, a jumbled collection of more or less spacious dug-outs, it would be sheer madness to walk on the top of the ground. Machine-guns are constantly playing across it, and at times the bullets flip through the air like a flight of birds. A number of troops are congregated here, but as long as they keep down they are fairly safe. Here, too, is the field dressing-station, and a row of canvas-shrouded figures lying on stretchers and looking exactly like mummies bespeaks the daily harvest of the trenches. They are waiting to be taken down to the Canal bank —and then carried away to the cemeteries.

It is awful work pushing and shoving along the communication-trench towards the front line, since with full bulk of equipment there is barely room for two to pass at a time. Hence long halts when everybody shouts "Make way! make way!" The men coming down from the trenches look jaded and worn-out. They have had a nerve-racking day and night, heavy shelling and many casualties. Like the wounded of the Twenty-first Brigade at Neuve Chapelle, "It is bloody Hell up there," they mutter; "the —— trenches are blown to bits." So they are, and far more than the greatest pessimist amongst us dreams.

The first sign of it is when we come to an immense hole right on the line of the communication-trench itself, utterly blotting it out. This hole would easily contain the foundations of a fair-sized cottage, and we have to work round and beyond it to discover where the trench begins again. Somebody grunts, "Minnie-wafer," and somebody else says "No, it's a big trench-mortar." Then I remember that this sector too has a sinister reputation for the most terrible engines of war; not the trench-mortar, which is to be expected, but the minenwerfer, that super-mortar which is one of the most frightful weapons the fiendish ingenuity of man has produced.

Beyond the crater there is a chain of brand-new 5·9 holes, and beyond these two more craters, one running into the other, after which the trench is virtually at an end. Here and there one may come upon a short length of sandbag breastwork still standing and a machine-gun post that remains practically intact. A shining moon reveals the ghostly naked walls of certain farm buildings which in days gone by clustered round a courtyard, and these now are the only key to distance and direction. Constantly, too, one meets stray parties of men just relieved stumbling thankfully to the rear. By mistake, as it were, one finds oneself in a short remaining section of the front-line trench. The rest—parapets, parados, dug-outs, sand-bags, communication-trenches—are utterly wiped out. One shell-hole succeeds another, clustering round some enormous crater in monotonous confusion; and were it not for the moonlight kindling the pools of water at the bottom, falls and involuntary wettings would be frequent.

The sentries and Lewis Gunners are at last relieved. There is no time to lose. Parties are immediately told off to go back for the rations and if possible to gain flank communication. The rest of the men sink down in one of the saps utterly wearied by their long walk. Everybody dreads stumbling by mistake into the German lines in the mysterious half-light. Fortunately all so far is quiet, but something sombre and foreboding seems to haunt the unusual stillness. Someone in my platoon remarks half-humorously, "The night is yet young, boys!"

We are back again in the line.

CHAPTER VI

DOWN TO THE SOMME

The days we had in the line next to the French were not so bad as our previous turn in the trenches. Indeed we were fairly fortunate in having such a few casualties. On July 18th (the day after we got in) I had one man killed and three men wounded by a shell, but apart from that, the total casualties otherwise for the Company during our stay were eleven men wounded and one man killed.

The Battalion, however, were very unlucky in officers. The Company Officer who got killed was out wiring in the front of the trenches. A star-light went up and, instead of throwing himself down, he stood still and got shot through the head.

Of the three Battalion officers, Lumsden was hit in the foot by a bit of shell, Howard was out wiring when the Germans crept up and threw some bombs and he got a few pieces in him; while Maynard was wounded in the head by a ricochet bullet. They have now all gone to Blighty, lucky devils—I find it is terribly tantalising to see people going off like that, but they had certainly earned it.

I take a particular interest in the Somme battles, as reported, since they are right down where the Entrenching Battalion was, and I know every inch of the country and all the places mentioned. We are now living in dug-outs by the Canal again—a very sepulchral spot.

The news has just come direct from Divisional Headquarters. The groups standing and lying about on the Canal bank get it first; then, like lightning, it flashes down the Yperlee and reaches the innermost recesses of every dug-out, and is even conveyed to the newly-brought-in wounded who are lying in the dressing-station dug-outs. Near Bridge Four it collects a crowd; at Blighty Bridge quite a number are discussing it half-an-hour after the first whisper has got abroad. By nightfall it has crept uncannily along the three-quarters of a mile of communication-trenches to the front line: it travels faster than any gas-wave. The only people who know nothing of it are the three canvas-shrouded figures lying side by side on stretchers in a *cul-de-sac*. And they will never know it.

"The Division is moving south!"

The news flies from mouth to mouth, and everybody congratulates everybody else. Everybody's heart leaps for joy because the dead weight of doom is lifted from their souls. The Salient is to be left behind, with its brown ditches, its impotence for the defenders, and—its implacable Fate. No more sitting still and suffering. There is to be a pause, at any rate, in the slow procession of the maimed, the dying, and the dead. There is to be a change of country, of scenery, of air, of habits. There is to be a long journey, long marching, gorgeous rests in remote places, quiet nights and still, lazy days, and a breath of Peace—and of Life. And at the end—who knows? Nothing worse than a battlefield on which one fights and lives or dies as men should, not lies in a ditch and waits for the inevitable end like dogs. Give us the first a thousand times! Make no mistake—Ypres gets on the nerves.

Twenty-four hours after hearing the news, and the day has come. A still, misty morning at the end of July resolves itself into brilliant sunshine and great heat. And as the first train leaves the railway siding near the old Poperinghe road, cheer upon cheer goes up to the blue sky. It is the men's farewell to Yperz, as they call it. "To the south!" They know that they are going into action—perhaps in a few days, perhaps in a few weeks—but this matters not a cuss: there is nothing but singing, laughter, and shouting to-day. For with every mile the hated Salient, the treacherous Canal-bank, the death-stricken city are left farther and farther behind. . . . The train rolls on. Its rhythm, its regular clank-clank-clank bursts into the great heat. By ten o'clock a broiling sun pours down its rays upon the young oak-woods beyond Proven, upon the flat fields and vegetable gardens and the fruit-laden orchards, upon the white highways whence clouds of dust rise. By road and rail to-day the relieving corps is moving up to Ypres. For many leagues—as far, say, as Wormhoudt—the railway line runs beside the road, and this road carries unending columns of perspiring, khaki-clad troops, unending lines of horse-transport and motor-lorries, unending columns of artillery—moving north. And they are fresh from the Somme, these dusty, heat-stricken warriors—at least thousands are left behind, and so many thousands are fresh from England—where they have been decimated. They are coming up here—for a rest! . . . God help 'em.

Wormhoudt is left behind, and with it the northward-bending army. One has a glimpse of three white roads converging on a wide, sun-baked square, which is full of troops. It reminds one of an Italian piazza, this Wormhoudt, where we had passed a showery eight days in June. I cannot quite see the old billets, the Flemish farm amid green, flat fields, with its heavy cows and brawling family of children that had seemed a Paradise then; but now the Hill of Cassel comes into view, and northward a wide vista of the Pas de Calais. A great undulating expanse of green fields and groups of trees and farms and cottages bounded sharply by a semicircular rim, and beyond this the blue ribbon of the Channel. At the edge of it, many miles away, a group of red-brick buildings surmounted by tall chimneys and a slight haze of smoke above that is Calais. And Gravelines is not far away, another little cluster of houses and chimneys right on the verge of the sea.

It is wonderful, this panorama, wonderful to us who for so long have seen nothing more spacious than Ypres viewed from the Salient on a clear day.

The detraining point has an unpronounceable name; it is also insignificant, being a mere sun-baked, sleepy railway yard without a square inch of shade. But here for the first time there is no sign of war. For the first time in many months one seems to leave the war behind, and as we march out into the country—a merry, chaffing, laughing column of schoolboys—no stench of motor lorries and petrol or swarms of troops greet us, but only the heavy silence of the woods and fields and villages, dreaming away their midday rest. A yellow cat strolls across the village streets, dogs lie basking outside the unsubstantial-looking inns—peculiar-looking dogs and very sleepy. Barely can they raise the energy to wag a tail at the flies which everywhere buzz and hum, creating with the drowsy heat an indescribable languor and murmur of summer. We halt in a shady oak-wood, and the men, recklessly happy, throw themselves down amid the long grass, the convolvuli, the straying honeysuckle. Yes, we are happy now, we who have suffered much!

And so at two of the afternoon, smoking, singing, and dust-covered, we march into billets. Everybody's thought is, God grant we stay here a while! For it is a lovely little village, like enough to those that one will find in Devonshire or Dorset, or that one will commonly find in France, with its old-fashioned thatched farmsteads and its cottages covered, many of them, with creeper, honeysuckle, and clambering roses.

In the afternoon the Company are paid in the farmyard in front of our billets, and later, towards evening, we take books and a deck-chair—hero of many vicissitudes this, and survivor of all!—out into the box-arbour and abandon ourselves to the dreamy stillness which steals over country places towards evening. We doze. The air is full of gentle sounds, alluring, restful: the drowsy hum of insects, the rippling notes of birds, of wrens, warblers, finches, the roo-coo-coo of a wood-pigeon in elms near the church, the purr-r-r of stock-doves, and presently the pleasant sound of an evening church bell.

After spending two brief days in this peaceful village, we left. The Battalion marched at dawn—a summery dawn that was shrouded in mists which presaged further great heat. Yesterday had been spent practically in idleness and resting, for the troops dozed away the hot middle hours, and only in the cool of the evening walked out into the country, watched the peasants working in the fields, strolled about, and looked at the gay village gardens.

By nine o'clock we were on the road again with a thirteen-mile march before us, and a long railway journey at the end. It was hoped to finish the march before the sun got up. Nobody minded the early hour, for the moist blue mists which blotted out the countryside and cloaked mysteriously the woods and fields were cool and delicious. Everybody felt fit, there was much laughing and singing as the Battalion swung along the dusty road. We passed through villages—old-fashioned and sweet-scented like the one we had just left—whose farms and cottages and inhabitants were yet asleep. Only an occasional farm-boy, milk-pail in hand, would come to the gate to see our long columns go by. But as the morning advanced and shafts of sunlight began to peep through the mists, people appeared at the gates of their cottages, at the cross-roads, and in groups and little family parties on their way to early church; which latter was the first intimation we had that it was Sunday, for in our vagrant stirring life of movement the days passed by almost uncounted. The halts were delightful, and more so as the noontide heat crept on; by the side of woods, shady and cool, on the edge of cornfields in lush grass, cornflower-starred and scarlet-splashed with poppies, on the village greens where the geese and turkeys wandered and the children gathered round, wide-eyed and curious. Out of the mists there peeped presently, now quite close, an ever-beckoning landmark, the Hill of Cassel, with its grey, old-world houses grouped on the summit. Thence one may see on a clear day Ypres and the dreadful Pilckem Ridge on the one side, on the other the sea about Nieuport almost to Ostend, and the ships in harbour at Dunkerque, and away to the south, Armentières and Merville and the dim Forest of Nieppe, westward the quiet villages of the Pas de Calais as far as that city itself.

We halted at the foot of the hill in fields close to the railway station. There was to be a three hours' rest in the heat of the day before entraining. The men ate their dinners—which had been cooking on the march—under the shade of some majestic elms, and a fine spread awaited us officers (previously arranged by a thoughtful quartermaster) at the farmhouse near by. This was followed by a smoke and a sleep, after which, the hour being about one o'clock, it was time to entrain. Cassel shimmered in the heat-haze; the sun scorched down upon a station-yard ankle-deep in dust. Two long trains stood in sidings, the engines with steam up; part of the Brigade had already gone on ahead. Here was to be seen a group of Staff officers—"red-caps," as the men call them—there a couple of *gendarmes* in black, silver-braided uniforms, and a few French railway officials in sky-blue. Once all the men were aboard, there was no waiting, and the train started on its sixty-mile journey at a good speed.

And what a perspiring, jolting, stifling journey it was! It rather reminded me of going home from school for the summer holidays. When the train stopped, as it occasionally did, there was no sound but the singing heat, and I listened for the familiar clatter of milk-cans, which is a thing inseparable from hot days at wayside country stations. But no such sounds came. Only the countryside, from being flat and ordinary at first, grew more and more Arcadian after we had passed through the tract of coal-mines and slag-heaps near Bethune and not far from Loos. After that, in the neighbourhood of St. Pol, came hills richly crowned with soft green woods, valleys and deep combes tumbling into one another, and full green hedgerows, and farmsteads and villages and grey or reddish lichen-grown church steeples peeping out from the dense foliage of trees.

The train ran through quickly, there were few stoppages, and in the late afternoon the detraining point was reached at a small and apparently remote country town. Anyway, it was over a dozen miles from the front. In the centre of the town, and near the railway station, on a grassy open space well shaded by elms, the men piled arms and had tea, while their officers found a repast waiting at the station buffet. There were boiled eggs and cold tinned salmon and salad, and coffee and rolls *ad lib.*, and jam and honey, and excellent omelettes and light beer—what more could the heart of man desire? Evidently troops had not passed through here in any great numbers.

Half-a-dozen stretchers in a row on the station platform, bearing recently wounded men, and a certain number of Red Cross ambulances arriving and departing, were the only signs that a battle was raging barely fifteen miles away. Otherwise the typical little French provincial town appeared as peaceful as any other place of the same kind in normal times. There were the *bourgeois* taking their Sunday evening stroll on the central boulevard, stopping and gazing with mild interest at the resting troops. There were the precocious French youths, with their vari-coloured bow-ties, their rakishly perched soft hats, and their canes carried in the hand, strutting about in parties, ogling the hatless girls, laughing, sporting, and showing off. Those who were not gathered in the boulevard were standing about chatting or playing leap-frog outside their houses.

When, soon after six o'clock, the Battalion fell in and marched out with bagpipes playing, there was naturally much excitement and gesticulation, for few of the local population had ever seen or heard the pipes before. A taxing march lay ahead, and the first lap of a gradient three miles long was the most trying part of it. Away in front, poplar-lined and straight as a ruler, the broad white road climbed ever and ever upwards. Sometimes it was obscured by clouds of chalky dust, sometimes it simply disappeared over the rim of the horizon into that golden land where the sun would presently set. Looking backward, we saw the little town which we had left an hour ago lying picturesquely in a dip of the hills, the blue smoke of its chimneys rising in a gentle haze.

What a different country, this, from the flat, closely cultivated small-holdings of Belgium! Rolling hills, crowned with woodland and scored with high leafy hedgerows, stretched away into distances infinitely dim and blue. It was God's own country this night. Not less wonderful because of the harvest which, more forward here than farther north, was strewn about the hillside fields and valleys in a wealth of stooks and sheaves. The reaper had done his work: the corn was cut and awaited carrying. Evening stole on, the rooks rose from the fields and wended their homeward way; from the grey village churches, hidden in combes and clefts, came the sound of bells. In this late summer scene there could be found no jarring note, but as the long, snake-like column mounted the last rise one divined a panoramic study of blue and gold untouched, unsullied by a hint of war. Blue sky, blue mists, blue distances, and greenish-blue tinge on the woods, and golden sunbeams sloping across the yellow stubble, kindling to a ruddy gold the wheat and oats.

At the start the march was noisy and boisterous, with the usual amount of laughter and singing, but after the first halt the men (who had already done a morning march) settled down to their work. It would take every man's utmost strength and determination to reach his journey's end. So, as evening fell and four miles of the journey had been covered, there was no more shouting and laughter, but the column tramped on in a silence that was almost grim. We passed through a large village with a long, broad, grass-bordered street, consisting of rather foolish-looking white-and-blue painted houses. The place was full of troops; another brigade had marched in only a few hours earlier. Beyond the village there stretched a great forest, which seemed to cover the surrounding hills.

When we entered the forest the sun had barely set, but under the great oak and beech trees, whose foliage arched over the road, forming seemingly an endless tunnel, night had already fallen. It was almost pitch-dark, and when after a mile or two we emerged, twilight had descended upon the world, and one could barely distinguish the hillside opposite. Here a halt was made, and it was pleasant to rest upon the bank in the cool dusk, watching the last embers of a gorgeous sunset die out of the sky. Close at hand, on the edge of the forest, no sound could be heard but the ceaseless chirruping of grasshoppers and crickets, the occasional croaking of a bull-frog in some distant pool, and the whoo-twhoo-whoo-whoo of an owl coming from the depths of the woods. Not far off was a railway, and the one lone lamp which stared out of the middle distance and the occasional whistle of an engine only served to emphasise the remoteness and solitude of the place.

Now it was completely dark, a thousand summery scents rose from the earth, the sky was bejewelled with stars, low down on the horizon a golden-coppery harvest moon, not yet at the full, sailed in the heavens. The night was indescribably contemplative; many and strange thoughts came to the mind. It is from this, this pageant of peace and plenty and beauty, that one goes into the bloody nightmare of battlefields. . . . What do the stars say, those stars so wise, so inscrutable? What do they say to each man who in such quiet moments asks himself whether, after all, this is not the end—of a life? Of how many lives? For many must travel the same road before the trees have lost their leaves. Nor do such thoughts bring with them forebodings or any "sadness of farewell," for in England are left behind the loves, the griefs, the hopes, the joys, the longings or regrets that make up the sum total of Existence and of Time. In France men think calmly of Death as of a thing ordained, knowing that it is ever near, knowing that for many the end of the road is their journey's end, not dreading or even allowing themselves to fear until the supreme moment comes, but ever wondering . . . and wondering.

Towards the middle of the night the men grew tired—so tired that they could scarcely stumble onwards in their fours. After many months in the trenches they had marched close on thirty miles in one day, and the effort was proving almost too great. But not a complaint was heard. At intervals of a mile or so, a footsore or utterly exhausted soldier sank down by the roadside and had to be carried the last lap on a transport wagon. He murmured, "I can't get any farther." However, the end of the march was near, and now the head of the column, after passing through a village which seemed to climb steeply a hillside, turned into an inky-black wood. Wooden huts were found, in which the men threw themselves down on bare boards without a word, and near by there was a farmhouse with court-yard and barn. After a cold repast quickly produced from the officers' mess-cart, we lay down thankfully to sleep, some in the living-room of the farmhouse, some on the floor of the barn.

Already the birds were awaking, and there was that deliciously fresh feeling in the air which comes just before dawn in summer. Already the cool grey light had begun to peep in through the open doors and windows of the barn.

That barn! It was a place of unknown horrors which in due course the glaring midday sunshine revealed. Black-beetles were crawling everywhere—black-beetles that fell from the wooden partition; black-beetles that crawled into and out of and under one's sleeping-bag and—yes, over one's prostrate body; black-beetles that did company or Battalion drill upon the floor under one's very nose. Hastily we fled the place, and next night slept in the farmhouse itself, but the memory of that rude awakening, I imagine, will long remain.

The farmhouse was a queer, ramshackle, untidy place, overrun with poultry, overgrown with weeds. It could not have been tended since the outbreak of war. Not less queer and untidy and dishevelled-looking were the tenants, a couple of frowsy old women and slat-ternly-looking girls, together with a smaller and numer-ous family. The men were apparently away; the old women quarrelled with frenzied shrieks and abuse like

London street-cats. The country around, one could see, was glorious, and in the village were many pleasant cottages, but the day after the march was too hot and one felt too languid to wander far. The only thing to do was to sit out in the deck-chairs or read in the shadiest part of the orchard.

At dawn the following morning another move was made through clinging mists which by eight o'clock had melted into scorching sunshine. On every hand one observed the glory of the harvest—the corn cut and standing in sheaves on the hillsides which sloped richly down the valleys from their wooded summits. Among the corn-stooks flitted flocks of finches, sparrows, and linnets; the yellow-hammers and crickets vied with each other in the beating out of an endlessly monotonous tune by the roadside. Overhead an unclouded blue sky—all the blue and gold and greenery of the year seemed to be concentrated in these early autumn days.

Of course the roads were ankle-deep in white dust; of course the distances were often very long and straight, and there was not always shade to be found at the halts. Already Ypres was forgotten, while the battle still seemed far away, and the war yet farther, so that there was the usual shouting and singing, and all marched well to the cheerful strains of the bagpipes. The villages, lying deep down in the trough of the valleys, looked curiously and utterly asleep. The inevitable dog slept head on paws in the middle of the road, the inevitable cat basked on a sunny window-sill or wall; at their cottage doors old women, with wrinkled yellow faces peering out of white linen sun-bonnets, might often be espied sewing. Somewhere, as one passed, the blacksmith could be heard beating out the sultry minutes on his anvil. Nobody troubled to come to the roadside to see the soldiers pass, for doubtless many thousands had tramped that way since the great southward movement of troops began.

And at the end of the march there was a "kit-strafe." Well, there would be on the hottest day in the whole year ! All the officers' sacks and valises were hurled remorselessly down on the roadside in the middle of the camp, and the Second in Command went through them one by one. There was no ceremony—my hair-oil newly arrived from England was sent spinning across to join a patent wash-hand stand, some books, some underclothes, a collapsible bed, a collapsible bath, and—my deck-chair. That chair, which had survived many marches, the rigours of Ypres, innumerable moves, substitutes, and evasions, had been the occasion of the most elaborate stratagems, was now solemnly sentenced to die an early death. "Folding chairs will not in future be included in officers' kit"—so ran the order. A chorus of protests was of no avail—the chairs were condemned not less than the hair-oil and the underclothes, and thereafter everybody was reduced to sitting on sugar-boxes or on roughly-knocked-up forms.

The camp at Bus lez Artois, which was our destination, was deep-hidden in one of those young oak-woods which abound thereabouts. Situated on the top of a hill, it was shady and cool, and, although there were wooden huts sufficient to accommodate all, everybody preferred to sleep out of doors while the fine weather lasted. Not many hours had been spent here before there came the first reminder of war since leaving Ypres. A German aeroplane, white and silvery in the sunshine, was observed travelling rapidly and very high up, pursued across the blue expanse of sky by three or four British planes. At night the thunder of the guns seemed to come very close, and going to the eastern edge of the wood, one could see a great shimmering in the southern sky to show where the battle raged.

The time that we have spent in this camp has been a time of unsullied enjoyment. There have been parades, marches, practice attacks, drill, physical drill, bayonet-fighting, schemes in the early morning, it is true, but there has been no war. After such parades the day's work was usually finished, except for an occasional evening march.

I have even had a day in Dunkerque, getting over there on a borrowed motor-bike; and a very nice old town I found it, with quite good shops. I had an excellent luncheon, and strolled round the harbour and port, and saw a lot of mine-sweepers, monitors, and torpedo boats, and it seemed quite funny being in a civilised place again.

Earlier this evening (August 4th) I biked over with Knollys to see some of the Bosche prisoners at a village near here. They were a very motley collection—some weedy and middle-aged, some very young, and some fine strapping chaps. Knollys talked to one or two in German, and they told him they came from central Germany.

The push seems to be going on all right so far, and it is at any rate consoling to know that the Bosches have not got a single division in reserve on this front. However, there is no doubt they fight magnificently and are very far from finished yet.

August 9th. This morning a party of Staff officers came unexpectedly round the camp, resplendent in gold lace, red caps, and blue or red-and-white armlets. The guard turned out—two faces seemed especially familiar, and everybody stood to attention. It was the King and the Prince of Wales. They stayed about twenty minutes.

It is August 12th and the powers that be saw fit yesterday to move us up to the trenches. As I write we are holding those in reserve, and go up into the front line to-morrow. By everything that I can see this is a very cushy place compared with the Ypres Salient; the trenches and dug-outs are deep and the Bosches quiet. Our artillery strafe unceasingly, but the Bosches do not reply much, though yesterday they sent over some tear-shells, and a lot of men came along the trench with tears streaming down their faces.

Just before we left camp, I had several more talks, *via* Knollys, with German prisoners (Bavarians). They impressed me greatly by their smartness and discipline, and many are very fine men in the prime of life. I talked, or at least Knollys talked, for some time with a Bavarian *Unter-offizier*. He said they expected Germany to win in three months. This was also his personal view before he was taken prisoner, but now he was not so sure. They disliked the English very much, he continued, but preferred to be taken prisoner by them, as they were treated better by us than by the French.

Rumour has it that Lord Cavan has got the First Army and Munro is going back to India. People seem to have a great and growing faith in Douglas Haig.

The weather remains very August—hot and still.

A fortnight has passed, during which time we have not been able to get any peace or quiet. Bad news has also come to me. I have just heard that my brother-in-law, dear old Jack Farmer of the 60th Rifles, has been killed in a show at Delville Wood. I don't know his Battalion or even his Division, but feel sure they are quite close here. Doubtless to-morrow I shall be able to find out all about it—where he is buried, etc. Poor Jack! He was a proper fine man.

Early last week I had a look round for Jack's Battalion, and found it in the next village. Unfortunately, however, unbeknownst to me it went back thirty-six hours later, so I failed to see the C.O. I am sorry about this, but I don't suppose there was anything of great value that I could have found out. I met one officer in Jack's Battalion who knew him, but he was attached to the Trench Mortars and had not been in the attack. I also saw the C.O. of the Ninth Battalion, who said they had a very bad time up at Delville Wood, and everybody coming back from there says the same. But I must still try and do my best to find the grave for my sister Angela's sake. Longueval, however, where Jack is buried, is constantly and heavily shelled, so it may not be possible to get up there by day; while by night it would be useless unless one knew the exact whereabouts of the grave.

Yesterday, September 2nd, I went up into the old German lines captured on July 1st. They had some enormous dug-outs. I also strolled around one of their cemeteries, which was not uninteresting.

The weather has been bad, with a lot of rain, but it is finer now, though unsettled.

The Colonel made a very handsome speech to me yesterday on the Battalion parade. He said, "Ewart, I have excellent reports of you, and I hear you are doing very well indeed. I notice you are getting much more self-confidence, etc.," and more likewise. This I suppose because I have been deputising for Stirling lately. We are kept very hard at work.

The cannonade is heavy to-day and there is a big battle on. The one cheering news in these troublous times is that our side is in a far better position now than ever before. There are very serious ideas of the whole German front going back to the line of the Meuse, and it is quite possible that we shall not go into it until that happens. Next door to us are the two best Divisions in the Army. The whole country behind the firing-line swarms with troops and artillery, and there can be no doubt now that we have a fine fighting army.

There is no chance of leave, I fear, until next month or even November, as there will be continuous fighting. However, ours in any case is a waiting rôle.

Indeed mine is a waiting rôle! In the last five days, while in Le Touquet on a Lewis Gun course, I have developed enteritis (poisoning from eating tinned food) and am in the Liverpool Hospital, Étaples, watching the September rains and accepting ministrations as my due. I am supposed to go back to the Battalion four days hence, on the 13th, but I shall not be fit by then. I feel pretty ill, but this is an excellent hospital; pretty well the best I have struck in this blessed war.

CHAPTER VII

YPRES AND CAMBRAI

How I spent my eleven months away from the front; how after leaving hospital in Étaples I went home, missing our taking of Ginchy Station and Lesboeufs by a few days and the Battalion's eventual return to Ypres; how I recuperated in Derbyshire and how, marked on my return "fit for home duty," I had my third spell of Wellington Barracks, all is of such little interest that I shall not describe it in detail.

I am now back in the Ypres Salient, and that to me appears an event of much greater significance.

I left London on Monday, July 30th, 1917. My journey was uneventful. I stopped only a few hours at Boulogne, and reached the Second Battalion, now commanded by Norman Orr-Ewing (who has succeeded Roger Tempest), on Wednesday, August 1st. The Battalion was in bivouac about three miles behind the line, in a horrible place, the rain pouring down, the earth a sea of mud. I went back to my old Company, G, and found Knollys in command. On Saturday, August 4th, the Battalion, which had come out of action the day I left London, went into the battle line again and I with them. It was my first taste of this lingering third battle of Ypres.

We had to cross the three thousand yards of ground

that had been captured in the former attack, and found the new line only partly dug in. There was a terrific and unceasing bombardment from the Bosches. We got badly shelled by our own people all through Sunday, and this, following the Bosches' bombardment of the night before, gave us a very worrying time.

On the Sunday night the Germans came out at us to try and blow up the bridge-heads across the river in front. They succeeded in blowing up one, and there was a lot of firing. Poor Esmond Elliot was shot through the body and arm a few yards from me, and his orderly killed outright. Esmond himself died about an hour later, having handed over his company to me. He was conscious almost to the last, and did not realise he was dying, though he was in great pain. I was left alone, and had a pretty hot time and several narrow escapes. At daybreak I got another officer up, but we had an anxious wait until relieved the following night by the Grenadiers. Esmond's funeral took place yesterday, August 8th. All the Divisional staff were there and most of the officers of the First and Second Battalions, including Knollys, Howard and Stirling.

We are now in rest camp several miles back—but only for a time—there will be plenty more fighting before long!

I have little to enter, as in the last fortnight since coming out of the line we have had quite an uneventful time. We will be going into the trenches again now almost at once, I hear, and I will command G

Company, as Knollys goes on leave—and commanding a company in the line will be some responsibility!

To-morrow, August 25th, the whole Brigade is going to be reviewed here at Poperinghe by the General Commanding the First French Army, Anthoine, and there is going to be a great show. This is in honour of the Brigade having fought next the French in the last battle, and the old boy is going to hand out Croix de Guerres and Légion d'Honneurs. There is going to be a march past, so we have been doing nothing but ceremonial drill for several days past—rather a pleasant change from the ordinary routine of training.

Two things in favour of this place are that on most afternoons I can go out riding, and that we have had here some lovely weather. It looks now, though, as if it is going to be windy and unsettled again.

I am in Paris! At the Hôtel Ritz, Place Vendôme. I have been trying to record an event or two for a fortnight past now, but owing to strange alternations of fortune it has not been possible. We went up into the line on Monday, August 27th, and only came out on Saturday, September 1st. The following day I got Paris leave, and I had a twenty-four hours' journey up here. Since arriving I have been leading a hurried, not to say hectic life. I return to the Battalion to-morrow night, September 7th.

We had on the whole a quiet time in the line, which was as well, as four days and five nights is a great strain. While I commanded Knollys' (G) Company we had not a single casualty, but on the contrary took a prisoner—a soldier of the 119th Grenadier (Wurtemberg) Regiment, who wandered into our outpost line and was promptly snaffled by a Lewis-Gun corporal. He was aged twenty-one, a native of Stuttgart, and quite a fine-looking fellow. I have got his watch and ring as souvenirs. We found on him rather an important message from a German outpost to an officer in rear, and he was carrying this when he lost his way.

My Company was given the job of throwing three pontoon bridges across a river practically under the nose of the Bosches, and this was done without being spotted, thanks to a light yet moonless night. F Company, next door, were not so fortunate. Markham, in command of a party, was spotted relieving outposts across the same river in bright moonlight, and the Bosches killed two of his party of four and shot him through both knees—a strong party of them then came out, and our remaining two men had to run back. They tried to hold off the Bosches, but their rifles were clogged with mud and they could not fire. Meanwhile poor Markham was lying propped against a tree between the two sides. A sergeant tried to bring him in, but he was in too great pain to be moved, so we had to leave him. Afterwards a Bosche was seen talking to him, but the following night when a patrol went out they could find no trace of him, so he is either killed or a prisoner.

Directly after coming out of the line, we had to change camp on account of shelling, and on Sunday night, as I seem to have written already, I left for Paris.

I stayed one night at Hazebrouck, whither the Bosches pursued me, as they made an air raid on the town that night, and I was awakened by furious anti-aircraft and machine-gun fire. Eventually I fetched up here, after travelling by a comic express from Calais. It was chock full of military of all nationalities, and stopped at every station up to Amiens. Here I found a lot of the Brigade and several officers I knew also on Paris leave, so we have all been going about together, and have had a very amusing time, sampling all the different fashionable places.

The weather has been lovely, though there was a heavy thunderstorm last night, and I am afraid the fine spell has now broken up.

On Tuesday we had luncheon at Henry's, where one is supposed to get the best food in Paris, drove in the Bois and down to Neuilly, and had tea at Les Ambassadeurs, which was crammed with a cosmopolitan, and chiefly military, crowd. Here we fell in with some very agreeable officers in the French Flying Corps, and spent a pleasant evening. We dined at Maxim's and went to the Olympia—both filled to overflowing with people of all nationalities. Yesterday we went for luncheon to a charming place in the Bois called Armenonville—tables out of doors and a delightful garden; not very many people, but excellent food. I only miss the bands. After this a drive through the Bois and tea at Ciro's, dinner at Ciro's, which was full, and a box at the Folies Bergères—a very good show with a lot of English stunts in it. Melville Gideon was there.

To-day, Thursday, I hope to see the American Ambassador hand over the American flag to the President at the Hôtel de Ville. I daresay it will be rather impressive; also I want to have a look at some of the picture-galleries, though I believe the Louvre is shut. The hotels in Paris are crowded, this one especially, but with nobody interesting except people in the Brigade. It is now time for luncheon.

It is very fine and hot here, and as flea-ridden a rest camp as one could find. I have been here now three days, which is to say since Saturday, when I arrived back from Paris. I enjoyed every moment of my leave except the journey each way. It was a very pleasant change. We move up in three days, I hear, but only, I think, to do fatigues. The Germans shell this place a bit, but the most serious thing are the raids at night. The Bosches come over then and drop bombs all round. In fact, they seem to be getting altogether too lively in these parts for comfort. Apart from them, though, there is little doing; one spends the whole morning drilling and in the evening generally goes out riding. To-day there was a drill competition between the companies with the Brigadier as judge, and it caused a good deal of rivalry, but such an event is about all that one can claim here as a happening.

Thursday, September 13th, 1917! It is a year to-day since I left Étaples for home. We are now in Abblingley camp and near the line. We moved up yesterday afternoon, shortly after it had been heavily bombed, so it is not a very healthy spot. When we arrived we found several Irish Guards and Garrison "Gunners" had been killed, and about twenty yards from the camp lay twenty-eight dead mules and horses all of a heap. The remaining wretched beasts kept calling for their friends all night.

We are in Brigade reserve here, and have carrying-fatigues to do up to the front line every other night—not pleasant, as the Bosche is too fond of shelling the roads. At the end of about eight days we are supposed to go back for a week or two, but Gawd knows what will happen after that!

As regards the general situation out here, reading the London papers, I rather gather that people in England have, as usual, got a false perspective of the position. The third battle of Ypres is admitted here to have been a failure so far, and there is now little more than a month of the "biffing" season left. We could hardly have gained less ground than we have, considering our enormous weight of artillery and superiority in numbers. But I am afraid much of our infantry is little better than the Bosches'. The latter have a pretty bad time from our guns, but everything points to the fact that they have plenty of men for the job in hand, or sufficient, and they fight every inch of the way. The Russian news, I read, is terrible. It looks like civil war. French officers have told me that they expect the war to go on at least two years. Personally I cannot now see how it can possibly be over one day sooner. The Bosches beat us in the air every time. I grow pessimistic, but I believe it to be true, alas! It is a fact that the situation twelve months ago looked actually better than it does now.

After a week of it, we go back to-day and farther back to-morrow. There are rumours of a few days on the sea-coast. The day before yesterday, September 18th, was a bad day here. The Second in Command of the First Battalion was killed by a bomb in his tent. He dined here the night before, and had only come back from hospital that day, after being wounded. The same afternoon an officer in the Fourth Grenadiers was killed by a shell. He was lying on a bank reading a book nearly five miles behind the line when hit. He was not killed outright, but badly messed about, and died shortly afterwards. Both had been out a very long time, so it was doubly bad luck.

Norman Orr-Ewing has just told me that he has recommended me to be made a captain at once, and if Knollys goes home for six months, I am promised his Company. The idea is that I shall command the Company through the winter and that Knollys shall come out again next April and relieve me. It is all a question, though, of what the Regimental Orderly Room in London say about it—and the chances are that they will jib.

I hear there is a chance that in ten days' time, on

September 30th, I may be sent on a Company Commanders' course. What ho!

I have been down here at the Fifth Army Infantry School a week now, and remain for another month, until November 4th. It took two days to get down from Belgium, an awful journey in cold trains crawling along the whole time. Fortunately I met a Grenadier officer I knew, going to a sniping course near here, and we travelled part of the way together. The weather was lovely until the middle of last week, but now has become awful—sheets of rain, wind, and rather cold.

We are well billeted here (I live in a room with three Grenadiers) and, of course, safe as houses; both of which are great compensations, but they work us very hard and the food is filthy, as on all courses. The fellows here are mostly captains and majors from every conceivable regiment, and we are all treated like privates—fall in the ranks, wear equipment, and carry rifles. One goes through practically the whole curriculum of modern infantry training, and we are on parade from 8.45 a.m. to 5.30 p.m., with a short interval for luncheon.

There are a lot of Yank officers here learning their job—very raw from America and very amusing, some of them; also very unsoldier-like, but not a bad lot on the whole, and much preferable to some of the T.G.'s.

"Our boys" have done well up the line, I see by the papers, and there does not look to be much left to do till next Spring, when, the Americans inform me, they expect to have one and a half million men and twenty thousand aeroplanes ready to fight in France.

Before leaving the Battalion I heard from Orr-Ewing that as he had heard my name *had* been sent in for promotion with some other people's in London, he expected me to be made a captain at once. This was nearly a fortnight ago, so I should be gazetted any day. About the six months in the Spring and my commanding G Company, I am less sanguine; I don't think now that there is the smallest chance of my getting it, for Knollys does not appear to be going home.

Well, so much for an entry. I must adjourn for dinner, where we shall doubtless discuss with animation how many bottles of beer a man can drink between dinner and breakfast.

This Army Infantry School would not be at all bad if the weather stayed fine. One learns a certain amount, and anyway ought to feel lucky not to be up in the line.

I get occasional trips to Amiens, which even in peace time is, I believe, one of the most agreeable cities in the whole of France. With a light-hearted atmosphere, an atmosphere of good food, good shops, and clean streets, it combines the cloistral simplicity of a cathedral town. It is the sort of place where everybody stays a night.

It is a curiously definite town. It does not straggle, but begins like a compact block of buildings, and ends, as it were, with the last house. One enters it by a long leafy boulevard full of children and nursery-maids—or rather those merry, hatless, shawl-covered girls who take their place in France, who wheel perambulators and herd babies. Immediately—leaving behind the *malaise* of the trenches, its flies and stinks, its indefinable atmosphere of stale war—one seems to enter there (how shall I say it?) the new zest, the holiday spirit. That—and a kind of friendliness and the renewal of acquaintance with civilisation—is what makes it so attractive to the man from the line. At first when I went there I felt strange, exotic, out-of-place. It was as though—in faded and very disreputable khaki—one had suddenly been dropped by an aeroplane in the centre of a great European city hundreds of miles from the war. It was as though after a long day's shooting one had strolled into a London drawing-room. At the same time, this is a very charming feeling. It is delightful to see men running about in billycock hats and dark clothes—even French billycocks; it is interesting to see trams and fashionably-dressed women and big bright shops. It is extraordinary to hear the sound of the trams—that indefinably civilised sound, with associations of the "Elephant and Castle" and the Vauxhall Bridge Road on wet days—of the *fiacres* rattling past, of the feet tapping the pavement, of the street-vendors selling newspapers and trifles.

Such crowds in the broad main street—it might be Paris in the height of the season, only there are more uniforms here. Everywhere the vivid sky-blue of the French officers; one feels that they might have stepped straight from the pages of *La Vie Parisienne*. It is Sunday, and for their visit to town they have put on all their crosses, medals, and what not. Most of them—especially the Flying Corps officers—are wearing four or five decorations. Occasionally I see dark green uniforms with gold facings—probably those of Engineers. *Poilus*, too, are numerous—*poilus* in tin hats, and sturdy little *Chasseurs Alpins*, with rakish tam-o'-shanters. Now and then I meet enormous negroes from the Colonial Corps wearing a kind of fez—great grinning fellows, standing six foot three inches, with broad flat noses and thick red lips; and Zouaves in short jackets and baggy *pantalons*. Belgians there are also, and, of course, a large sprinkling of English khaki. Here comes a Sikh on horseback. To this varied throng, Australians with their slouch hats, and Canadians, all coppery-faced and sun-tanned, bring a suggestion of far-distant climes.

Civilians, smartly dressed little ladies in the latest from Paris, showing plenty of open-work stocking and shapely limb, trip along in twos and threes, naïvely laughing and exchanging jokes—always laughing. Soberly-dressed, comfortable-looking gentlemen carrying heavily-tasselled umbrellas, wife on arm—some wife!—are taking their Sunday morning promenade; they bow to each other solemnly across the road. Doubtless they are the chief tradesmen or municipal officials of the town. The trees of the gardens at the farther end of the main street look green and cool, and a number of people are strolling beneath them or sitting contentedly on the seats. There is even to be seen that delightful and unchanging Frenchman who, since the beginning of time, has sat under the trees of a public garden, reading a newspaper.

Nor is there any lack of wheeled traffic. The main street simply shrieks with it. Enormous motor-cars, usually containing English or French generals or French Flying Corps officers, constantly rush past at breakneck speed, hooting furiously. *Fiacres* rattle briskly over the cobble-stones; motor bicycles add greatly to the noise of the thoroughfare and do their best to knock everybody down within reach; bicycles—without which no French town would be complete—tear in and out among the other vehicles, creating by their frantic bell-ringing a special frenzy of their own. Although it is Sunday, most of the shops are open, and their coloured awnings in the brilliant sunshine lend a summery aspect to the scene. Already the *cafés* are crammed and—quite in the dear old manner of Versailles or the Avenue de l'Opéra—crowds sit at the marble-top tables amid the little orange trees, or out on the pavement, sipping strange coloured drinks. Hard to think as one looks down the street, so gay, so sunny, that not so very long ago Amiens was in the hands of the invader! Hard to think that not twenty miles away one finds the silent, stink-ridden, death-stricken world of the trenches. Ah, well! they deserve their fun, these *jeunes hommes*. At the same time, one has the fancy that here in this motley cosmopolitan throng—not in London or Paris or Petrograd—is the living hub of the world to-day.

After drawing the necessary amount of money at the bank and indulging in a hair-cut and a shampoo, a friend and I repair to the Mecca of subalterns, the

Hôtel du Rhin. Now, there is a choice of several hotels in Amiens, and some prefer the Belfort or its rival next door. For my part, however, I have no doubt about the Rhin. Here one gets not only an excellent luncheon and excellent wines, but one is amused, which, after all, is the best appetiser. Yes, one gets a luncheon as well cooked as any ever eaten at the Carlton or the Ritz. There are melon, *hors d'œuvres*, fish or *omelette*, beef-steak or *poulet roti*, and *glacé*, or anything one likes to follow. The place is full of officers, French and English, but chiefly the latter. Never was an Amiens hotel so animated in ordinary times. At a table near by sits a merry party; some young Frenchmen have brought out their wives or sweethearts, and they are all chattering at once amid peals of laughter. One or two widows may be seen in the peculiarly becoming black costumes of their country. Not far away a couple of Parisian ladies are sitting; one can pick them out in a moment by their dashing hats, their very short and wide frocks, their indefinable air of enterprising *chic*.

We drink coffee on a verandah that looks out over a pleasant shady garden, then return to exploration. There is much shopping to be done. The chocolate shops in Amiens are irresistible, and one cannot depart in peace without buying some of the delicious "roc" that literally melts in one's mouth. To all outward appearances the town is precisely the same as ever, even to the pigeons and jackdaws which circle about the Cathedral or chatter raucously from its numerous pinnacles. Only when one walks round to the front one discovers that that wonderful façade is completely sand-bagged up. Within are to be seen the usual small parties strolling round, but most of them now are composed of English or Colonial soldiers. At the side of the great Cathedral, where in a patch of rank green grass lie many lichen-grown slabs of stone, tomb-heads and the like, it is pleasant to watch the play of sunlight on the old grey sacristy and to imagine oneself a tourist again. Such a corner could belong to almost any cathedral close of England or France.

Having seen the chief *spectacle* of the place, we visit the shops again, and then sit awhile outside a *café*, watching the endlessly varied human stream flow by. After tea we hire a *fiacre* and drive ponderously but happily round the outskirts from side to side of the road at the nag's pleasure. It is pleasant thus to clatter through some of the narrow, cobbled, old-fashioned streets where the houses, white, pink, and pale green, huddle together in crooked confusion. Here one has a different atmosphere from that of the Grande Rue. The *gamins* run beside the chaise, calling for coppers, and somehow the green venetian shutters, the snatches of song, and the whiffs of garlic that come from high narrow windows, remind me of Italy. So do the twisting straightness of the streets and the hatless young women strolling arm-in-arm with the sallow dark-eyed young men. Then it is pleasant to pause on the outskirts of the town by the river where the tall poplars stand in rows, and to watch the level evening sunbeams light up the green flat country beyond; boats rock lazily on the river, people are wandering beside it or lying sleepily about on the banks; it is such a peaceful scene that I might fancy myself in, say, Cambridge, at mid-summer.

Dinner at the Rhin is a gorgeous meal. The place is packed and brilliantly lighted, and the atmosphere one of great hilarity. Most of the people who were at *déjeuner* are here again. The champagne is excellent, and if towards the end of the evening some of the company have obviously had enough of it, well, that is surely the proper spirit in which to face a drive. Nobody feels depressed, therefore, when soon after ten o'clock the moment comes to leave these gay scenes and to go out into the inky darkness. Everything is silent and deserted now, scarcely a footfall echoes along the street, while far away in the eastern sky I see the old familiar flicker of the guns.

The car carries us swiftly towards them.

I leave the Fifth Army Infantry School in twelve days' time, as expected, on Sunday, November 4th; but I do not yet know whether I shall then have to go up to the Battalion or whether I shall get my English leave. I shall not be sorry to leave here. Five weeks of such a strenuous existence is quite enough and it has grown rather monotonous. Three days ago, on Sunday, October 21st, I had a very interesting day with an American. I went up to the Somme battlefield, which is about twelve miles from here, and traversed all the most famous places. It is an awful spot, and even now a lot of stuff is lying about, and it looks like one great cemetery, a regular forest of crosses. I spent a long time looking for the place where Jack was killed and may be buried, but every landmark—roads, houses, villages—being utterly blotted out, I could only find it eventually by map and compass near sundown. It was then too dark to find his grave among so many, but I now know exactly where to look for it, and hope to go up there again before I leave this region.

News has just come that an officer in my Company was killed in the Second Battalion's last show on the fifteenth. This, following upon Esmond Elliot, is very sad. The First Battalion had three officers killed, one of whom came out with me this last time. It is a toss-up what is going to happen to us next!

It is Saturday, December 8th, 1917, and six weeks and three days since I made an entry. What a world of experience I have had in this short time! Early in November I went on leave—home to London, and on November 22nd rejoined the Battalion. Since then I have been through some arduous, not to say unpleasant times. I have been through the whole of the Cambrai show with nothing worse than sore feet and a few bruises, and though in a fortnight I have only once changed my boots or taken my clothes off, so far I have only had a slight chill as a reward. Here then is a recital of my life and my sufferings.

On joining the Battalion on November 22nd after leave, I found them south-east of Bapaume, just moving up to the battle, having done some long marches from the north. Everybody was full of wild rumours as to our having broken through beyond Cambrai, and of the Bosches running before the tanks and cavalry; most of them, needless to say, not true.

At daybreak on the 23rd we marched about eight miles, camped during the day in great discomfort, and marched another eight miles that night across the Hindenburg Line (which was captured on the 20th) to some good German dug-outs on the fringe of the battle. In the morning we found ourselves in front of Bourlon Wood and saw the church spires of Cambrai, five miles to the south-east, the Germans heavily shelling the neighbouring villages of Graincourt and Anneux, and our knocked-out tanks lying about in all directions. The wounded were pouring back. At nine o'clock that evening the order came to move up to Bourlon Wood, which we did as a Battalion, getting shelled a bit going across the open. Bourlon Wood was a nightmare sort of place—pitch dark and no one knew its tortuous ways or quite where the Germans were. It is a big wood divided up by rides and summer roads. After going half-way through it, very heavy rifle and machine-gun fire broke out in front on the farther edge of the wood, lights going up all round. Several men got hit, and down the ride there came a surging mob of cavalrymen, infantry, and engineers absolutely out of control, shouting and yelling that the Germans had broken in and were coming through the wood. It was a fine example of New Army discipline. Our men fixed bayonets, lined the ride, expecting every moment a terrific German onslaught. Nothing happened. We then went on through the wood, which was pitch dark, nobody knowing whether the Bosches had been driven out or not, and eventually dug in. We then found some very windy Highlanders and dismounted cavalry, and we got orders to push on and drive the Bosches out at daybreak. This of course was sheer open fighting, and quite different from anything we had done before except on field days. As soon as it got light the three companies advanced in extended order, and it was not long before the bullets began to fly, and Howard's Company got hung up by machine-guns on the left. Consequently we could not get on. Desultory and sometimes very sharp fighting went on for about two and a half hours. We sniped a lot of Bosches. Then Howard got badly wounded, and it was obvious the Bosches were too strong for us. As a matter of fact we afterwards heard that the north-east part of the wood was held by two Battalions of the Third Prussian Guard Division and must simply have been swarming with them, so we could hardly expect to take it with three companies. Later in the morning we were told the Bosches must be cleared out at all costs, and we had to attack again at two o'clock, with the First Guards Brigade on our right. This was at 1.15, so there was not much time to arrange it, and I had the wind up as never before, feeling certain that it was impossible to take the place owing to the machine-guns which were supposed to be rushed with the bayonet, but which nobody really knew the whereabouts and number of. We lined along a summer ride and went over just at the tail end of a sleet-storm. There was a short and quite useless machine-gun barrage, no artillery. Just after we had gone over, Tyringham tried to stop us, as the Command realised the hopelessness of it, but it was then too late. F Company got ahead on the right and I heard a lot of firing. Sergeant Fotheringham, a chap I got the D.C.M. for at Ypres, was with me, and he kept bringing the men on in the most magnificent way, and he was wonderful from first to last, and if he had lived would have got a V.C. or bar to his D.C.M. When we got to the more open part of the wood I saw what had happened—just as I expected. Menzies, the Company Commander, and Sergeant Maclean with all the leading men of F Company had been laid out together trying to rush the machine-guns. At the same moment the two machine-guns slewed round on to us, and I realised that we were only about fifteen yards from one of them. Of course we flung ourselves down, Sergeant Fotheringham, a man called Grant—the same that was wounded at Neuve Chapelle—in F Company, and myself; and for the next twenty minutes there was nothing but a young oak-tree between us three and eternity. The machine-gun fired absolutely point blank, but could not quite reach us on account of the tree. Most of the platoon got down in a depression about twenty-five yards behind, but about eight men, including two Lewis Gunners, were almost up with us. These kept on firing for all they were worth, and the Lewis Gunners working their guns in the open until they were killed. Every man was killed one after the other, and Grant is the only man left alive besides myself. Then the Bosches started throwing phosphorous bombs at the dead and wounded, which set light to them and burnt them up. I thought I had seen most of the nasty things in this war, but this was the nastiest by a long way. By this time the rest of the men had retired, but we three were still lying behind the tree, unable to move an eyelid. However, after about twenty minutes the Germans got tired of shooting, and we decided to get away if possible one by one. Grant went first, and got across the open all right, though fired at from each side. Then Sergeant Fotheringham volunteered to try and get one of the Lewis guns away. He had his arm shattered at once, but managed to crawl back, only to die at the dressing-station. He was a great friend of mine and I feel his loss very much. I waited about five minutes and then did a lightning sprint on my stomach, and by all natural laws ought to have been hit—the bullets were knocking stones up into my face. However, I got back in the end. It was an experience I shall never wish to repeat, and it is no compensation for the loss of people like Menzies, and Sergeants Fotheringham and Maclean to know that what they were asked to do was absolutely impossible. It is little consolation even to know that the Corps General has been sent home.

That night we got relieved by a line regiment and went about four hundred yards back in support. Next day I was transferred to command F Company with one subaltern, who got badly shell-shocked the same night, so I was then left alone. Later, another subaltern was transferred from G Company to me. We were relieved by the Second Irish Guards, who got it in the neck from a 5·9 barrage coming up and we escaped it by luck. After a day in reserve dug-outs we marched back six miles and had a day's rest.

The next day we were supposed to go out for a month's rest, but about breakfast-time the great German counter-bombardment began, of course a long way off, and within an hour we were on the road again, with men and transport fleeing on every side, roads absolutely choked. No time to get into fighting kit—I had my best uniform on, not the least annoying part of the business. The whole of at least one Division were running for their lives, and the chaos was indescribable. About one o'clock we halted in open country, the whole Third Brigade, got into artillery formation, and the Brigadier, who was on the spot, ordered an advance until we came into contact with the Bosches, who were supposed to be on top of us at any moment. Every ride and rise we expected to meet them. As a matter of fact they had already been held up by the First and Second Guards Brigades on right and left. I think no one will dispute that the Guards Division saved the day on this occasion, at any rate. The rest were nowhere. Well, at midnight the whole Division was ordered to counter-attack with tanks and cavalry. This was afterwards changed to daybreak. We were in Brigade reserve and lost very little; my Company, being the weakest, was in battalion reserve, but the Fourth Grenadiers and Welsh Guards had an awful time. Next night my Company moved up into close support on the railway line, where we got badly shelled and had several casualties. I took over from King's Company First Grenadiers. Though nothing else happened, it was an unpleasant time, as we expected a counter-attack at any moment and kept on standing-to. The S.O.S. went up twice in one afternoon, and warnings kept on coming from the Brigade that the Germans were coming over the ridge. However, in the end we never got an attack at all. Then, after ten days' fighting and hardship, by far the worst I have had to endure since the war began, we were relieved and came back eight miles, where we waited thirty-six hours for a train which eventually brought us right back here—a journey of twenty-two miles, taking eight hours in cattle-trucks, owing to the line being blown up!

This is a nice quiet village and we are in good billets, but it does not look as if there is going to be much rest as far as I can make out.

Nine days have passed. The weather has turned vile, and at present the ground is covered with damp snow, and it is correspondingly cold. Fortunately we remain in our excellent billets for the time being. Yesterday I went on a motor trip to the neighbouring town of Arras and had a couple of hearty meals, but it was a bitterly cold thirty-five-mile drive coming back.

All the men I recommended for the Cambrai show, I now hear, have got the Military Medal, except their Corporal, who is going to get the D.C.M.

Must now go and inspect rifles—through the driving snow!

Six days now to Christmas. I expect to spend it in good billets, as we are pretty sure to be out of the line this year, not like my other war Christmas, in the trenches after a *rencontre* with the Bosches. The weather at present is still very cold and wintry, but bright.

Several people have sent me things already—a plum-pudding, a tinned chicken, a cake, a diary, a cigarette-lighter, and an Orilux torch;—this last especially will be invaluable.

Lord knows when my captaincy comes. I have given up thinking about it, having only just realised that one's C.O.'s word can no more be relied on than anybody else's. And I saw the original thing in writing!!

We have managed to spend quite a cheerful Christmas. There was a Battalion Dinner with the usual amount of drinking and shouting, and last night, December 28th, we feasted off a goose. There was also a sergeants' concert, a fearsome orgy. They all got blind to a man, and everybody's health had to be drunk in whiskey punch. One blighter kept shouting out: "Good old Mr. Ewitt! Good old Mr. Ewitt! He led me over the top," but personally, I could not remember the occasion.

To-day I went down to Divisional Headquarters, and to-night I have got two Grenadiers coming in to dine. Our rest here will be short-lived, but I am going on a four days' course of Wireless Telegraphy, which will mean my missing the next go of the trenches. Doubtless, I shall have enough visits next Spring—and to spare!

CHAPTER VIII

ARRAS TO THE ARMISTICE

Here—on this Wireless Telegraphy course which is absolutely useless—things jog along pretty quietly. The Battalion is in the trenches at present, but I am left out for the first eight days, it being my turn. I go back, however, on Wednesday. The line—a few kilometres from Arras—is very good and very quiet at present, I hear; but of course our people always insist upon waking things up. I went up to the reserve line to-day (January 7th), and only heard about four shells burst all the time I was there. I am going up for seven days, I think, on the 10th, after which I hope to get Paris leave, though this is not at all certain. It will be expensive, but it makes a delightful change, and is a temptation I can't resist.

The cold is, and has been, terrific for over a fortnight; far worse, I am told, than in England, and there is still snow on the ground. But of course it is dry. I enter this in at the very good officers' club we have here, where most people foregather.

January 15th, 1918. I am writing this in a dug-out in the support trenches, where we are pretty comfortable on the whole, although sixteen days at a time gets a bit monotonous and one gets practically no exercise. The line, however, is very quiet at present, while the weather, except for occasional snowstorms, has been splendid. But now, I am afraid, it is turning to rain, although it is much warmer.

At the end of the week I hope to get my three or four days in Paris, but this leave is not so easy to get now as it was.

We move into the front line to-night.

I have tried to write for a fortnight, but it has been impossible with so much to do, and I am at present looking after the Company.

Things go on as usual here. My Paris leave did not materialise, as a brother officer was sent on a course at the last moment, which left me in charge of the Company. We are at the present moment in reserve, and go into the front line a night or two hence.

I rode up to the trenches to-day (January 28th) to make the necessary arrangements. They are pretty good, and the Bosche keeps quiet at present, but sixteen days, I still maintain, is a lot to do at a time. Life in dug-outs, indeed, becomes more than a bit trying. During the last "tour" the rain brought the trenches tumbling in, and the mud was so bad they simply could not be used. The Germans and ourselves were walking about on the top in full view of each other, neither side wanting to shoot. The other afternoon I rode up to the Vimy Ridge. It is a steep place on the German side with a wonderful view on a clear day across to Lens and Douai. The weather has been delightful for the time of year, and I am keeping fairly fit except for an inability to sleep at night.

Last night, February 9th, we gave a dinner to the Fourth Grenadiers, who are leaving the Brigade at once under the new re-grouping scheme. It was a proper orgy, and every one got tight; but it was great fun, and we are sorry to lose them.

Leave has gone phut, and I shall not get mine before the 4th of March at the earliest, though it is really due ten days from now. However, I hear to-day that I have been recommended for six months' light duty in England under the new scheme by which officers who have been out here some time are sent home for a rest. As I have been out altogether longer than any other subaltern and been over the top three times, it takes me first in this Battalion. Whether I shall get it is another matter, as there is some idea that one has to have completed two years, and I have not quite done that yet.

The C.O. sent for me after the last go in the front line, and said he was extremely pleased with the way I had commanded the Company, and that he intended to recommend me very strongly again to be made a captain at once. He thought it disgraceful that I had not been promoted before. I think so, too, as I have been doing chiefly captain's work, and I am a fool not to have agitated before about it—but I intend to now.

At the present moment I have got violent neuralgia and a very slight touch of influenza. However, I expect I shall be all right by to-morrow. Often I feel extraordinarily weary and that they have had the best out of me. I cannot look forward with confidence to any more battles.

I read that the air-raids in England seem to have been rather bad lately and the food situation still worse. I have just heard also that my sister intends becoming a W.A.A.C. I hope to heaven someone stops her. I saw some in Amiens when last there, and they gave me the face-ache. They ought to be warned off the street anyway, for all their noble work.

I feel I cannot stand this life any longer. My leave is a month over-due, and it seems interminable waiting for it. A Bosche attack is expected hourly and we live in a state of great tension—in the line all the time and apparently no prospect of a rest yet. That, like my leave, is long overdue.

We are at last out of the line, but we go back in a day or two. My leave seems farther off than ever. I have had it in my pocket for a week, but am not allowed to go, as I am in charge of the Company and there is still a tremendous wind-up about the German attack. It is pretty rotten luck with everybody going ahead of me, but I suppose I must just bear with it.

The great German attack is supposed to be so imminent that we return to the line in " battle formation." But I daresay it is largely "wind."

The weather still remains lovely.

Five or six weeks passed! The 22nd April! Well, The explanation is that I have been away on leave, missing the fourth battle of Arras. Add to that the fact that I have at last got my captaincy and it appears my luck has changed.

I am at present in a quite nice village, Barly, some miles back, and have not been in the line since my return. Of course we are now liable to move up at any moment. However, the Division had a very long and trying spell in the trenches while I was away, so they ought to give us a week or two's rest. The situation looks dangerous everywhere at the moment. The Bosches are practically certain to attack again down here soon. A very great deal depends on what they do in the next day or two north of Bailleul. If they get the high ground there, Ypres has to go, and we will all have to go back some way. But both we and the French still have big reserves, which I suppose will be thrown in at the favourable moment. At the same time the Bosche has enormous reserves, and we shall have to fight like grim death to hold him.

I hear that there is a chance of my getting the Military Cross for Cambrai. The C.O. told me that I was put in for it in December, but most of our honours were washed out, and he now says I have been put in again, and he hopes I'll get it in the Birthday Honours. This is all news to me, as I have never heard a hint before.

Must stop scribbling to go to a football match.

April 24th. Yesterday I attended a court-martial, a responsible and rather unpleasant business, and to-morrow night I go into the front line for, I expect, a week.

I have just been offered the job of liaison officer with the French. It just depends on how well I can get along with the language. Of course, I can speak very little. However, one can but try, and it would probably be very interesting.

In the last three weeks little has happened. I am still waiting for a "job" to materialise. It appears no easy matter to get one unless one has direct personal influence. The liaison job has come to nothing so far, and in any case I am not sure that I should be competent for it. I am still out of the line, but go up again for a spell two days hence, on May 16th. Warlincourt is a charming village to be in. Very pretty and quiet, not too full of troops. My tent is pitched in an orchard overlooking a wooded valley, and during the fine weather it has been very pleasant lying out all day. An officer in this Battalion who has been some time with us was unluckily killed the other morning—shot in mistake by one of our own sentries: though not the sentry's fault, however. I went to Abbeville for the day recently and got a tolerably good meal, but it is a longish way from here. Otherwise I have little to record. I lead a more or less monotonous life. All leave is stopped, of course—it was stopped on March 21st—with no prospect whatever of its starting again yet awhile. No Paris leave either. It will reopen when the battle is over—but that is, God knows when.

The situation is stationary at present, but I gather there is no great confidence about the future in high quarters. The Bosche will push at any moment and will take a deal of holding. The Yanks, however, are arriving in considerable numbers.

I have been in the line eight days—since May 16th—and things are fairly quiet at present. It cannot be long now, though, before the battle breaks out again.

As I am last but one in the Battalion when leave starts, I have quite given up any thought of it. I should think October would be my very earliest chance, as even when it starts, it is sure to go very slowly for some time.

Our fortnight before coming here was a delightful rest. Perfect weather, very pretty country, riding every evening. The only fly in the ointment was the bombing at night, which often came unpleasantly close. Indeed, at the next farm to us one night just before we left four Grenadier officers were knocked out—three killed and one wounded, which was rotten luck.

We have had several casualties lately—two officers killed and three wounded.

I seem to be as far off as ever from getting a job. Even the liaison thing has apparently fallen through.

I was wrong in my entry of May 23rd, eighteen days ago; the liaison job has not fallen through after all. I have just been appointed G.S.O.3 (General Staff Officer 3rd Grade) to a Division with the 36th French Army Corps (liaison) and am off immediately. I am pleased to think it will be an interesting job. Am starting for the North to-morrow.

Abbeville station at ten o'clock of a sultry June morning, waiting for the Paris express, is a busy place. All is noise, clamour, and vociferous energy, as might be expected of one of the chief railway centres behind the Western Front. A hooting of sirens, a blowing of horns, a backing in and out of long supply and troop-trains, a shouting and a crying of railway officials, a wild bustling and wrestling with luggage, R.T.O.'s and the Mission Militaire. And what a crowd on the station platform! The uniforms of all the Allies seem to be here in one representative gathering; and the photographer, the cinematographer—where are they? Certainly the predominant note is khaki—the khaki of the heavy and solid English, the square, thick-set English with their unromantic, imperturbable calm; of the Americans, lithe and slim, rather like keen commercial travellers, with nasal voices, odd cynical faces, and an air of being perpetually amused; of the Belgians, bearded, learned, new-looking, too new-looking, with their bright yellow boots and belts. The requisite dash of colour is found among the French officers, who, in sky-blue of the smartest, rush wildly hither and thither. And there are many *poilus* in steel helmets and rather battered uniforms going on *permission* or returning therefrom. On the platform opposite is a group of Portuguese in grey uniforms, whose dark sallow complexions speak of Oporto, orange-groves, and the sun-baked South. There are Australians and Canadians, quite another but equally well-known type, and standing by himself a little Japanese of the Staff. Behind all these the background of the crowd—the demure-looking V.A.D.'s, grip in hand, the severer hospital nurses. A motley collection, a curious *spectacle* in the fierce sunshine.

Then the Paris train comes in. The scene is indescribable—the confusion, the rushing to and fro, the perilous shifting of luggage on trucks, the blowing of horns and of whistles. In a first-class compartment are found a middle-class Frenchman and his wife, the owner of a factory and brickfield near the coast—a prosperous-looking couple with charming manners and execrable clothes—who are returning from a visit to their property; a reserved, white-haired civilian Englishman, for twenty years resident in Armentières as agent of a big British firm—thoroughly commercial; a French *jeune personne*; and myself.

Through all the long and sultry day the train rolls on its circuitous way towards Paris—faster, mercifully, than that of yore. First it touches the sea, then turns inland, passing through a rather monotonous country whose broad marshy valleys, traversed by streams, are bounded by low and often wooded hills. The meadows are richly clothed with cowslips, buttercups, and marigolds; on the folding woods is a still spring-time green, the corn, ripening visibly, waves in the wind, whilst flippant magpies—those typical birds of Northern France—flit from tree to railway embankment and back again. The journey, though wearisome, is not without diversion. At *déjeuner* in the restaurant car a French infantryman sits opposite reading *La Revue de Paris*! (Can one imagine an English Tommy reading the *Hibbert Journal*?) He has been gassed, this erudite fellow, I learn, in the fighting at Kemmel, has just been discharged from hospital, and is on a week's leave to his home in the Midi. Every hour or two the train stops at some station of mediocre importance, whereupon we all clamber out to walk up and down, talking and smoking, beside the line.

At Abancourt many descend. At Beauvais the remainder make an exodus to the dining-car. I nod. I doze.

Paris!

Paris in the gathering dusk of a sultry June evening. The German armies are forty miles away. . . . Is there any sign of this in the roar and bustle of the Gare du Nord, in the whirl of humanity that seems to press convulsively without, in the surging tide that sweeps through the swing doors and besieges every mode of conveyance and stands in queues and waits patiently in throngs and crowds? Yes, there is. One portion of these crowds and throngs is seeking a way out of the threatened city; but by far the larger portion are immigrants, refugees, who, hurriedly evicted from villages and farms in secluded country places, are cast high and dry upon the metropolis by the current of war, roughly handled, swirled in the whirlpool of humanity they know not whither. Of such is this group of old women and children marooned amid their baggage; these nuns, sad-looking in their silent resignation, sitting on little packages, clasping old-fashioned, shabby umbrellas; these middle-aged women and youths rushing frenziedly between soldiers and officials in vain search for transport and information. What a pandemonium! What a world of dreariness and weariness beneath the dim arc-lights that compete with fading sunset under the great vault of the station roof!

I pass out of the station into the now dim and purple dusk; a glowing orbit of electric light enclosed by a mob of interested faces detains me. It is like a glimpse of some episode on a brilliantly lighted stage. Within the blaze of electricity the refugee children and the parentless babies are being tended by nurses, Samaritan-like, in miraculous white. There are cots and beds and an atmosphere of eager solicitude. At least, so it seems—but the crowd presses ruthlessly on, and it is possible only to treasure gratefully in the mind this vision of American charity.

Out in the streets there is felt something of that electric atmosphere which brooded over the streets of London on the evening of August 4th, 1914. The people ebb and surge, there is an indefinable air of crisis, of expectancy, so that the mind goes back wonderingly to the rippling Authie river and the stricken streets of Abbeville, where last night scarcely a footfall echoed.

Morning again, and in its bright light the garden of the Hôtel Ritz in the Place Vendôme looks cool, exotic, and exceedingly peaceful. The hotel is all white, and smiles in the gay sunshine. There is a glimpse of a glass verandah, a gravel walk, and one or two beds of flowers, and groups of palms and orange trees in boxes, and a fountain playing; and of numerous little green tables set about in shady places. With its twittering sparrows, its trickling flow of water, its pattern-work of light and shade, one could find no pleasanter spot to look down upon at this early hour. And there are two waiters. There are two waiters dusting tables, rearranging chairs, tidying the place up—and a head waiter superciliously looking on—in such a manner that they somehow create for themselves an atmosphere of lazy peace quite peculiar to the waiter-world!

It would be difficult to find a more pleasant experience than such extreme luxury after months of plain living or of hardship. There is nothing more delightful than a French breakfast in a comfortable bed, a feeling of *abandon* and of liberty to lie long, and looking out into the cool courtyard, a leisurely getting up, and a leisurely dressing. A hot bath—no! That is impossible. In Paris they bathe only on Saturdays and Sundays.

Then the streets—everything twinkles, laughs, and shines this summer morning. The great hotel itself is strangely quiet. It is empty save for a gorgeous *concierge*, a polite mysterious gentleman in a tail-coat, a hovering waiter, and one or two American officers sauntering in and out. None of the swarms of English khaki that were here nine months ago. That same note is lacking in the streets. These do not want for movement, animation, colour, for motor traffic, and for shops fully and brilliantly open. But they lack a kind of mainspring, a kind of dynamic energy, a characteristic *joie de vivre* that was of Paris when I was here before. Appearances, nevertheless, are deceptive. They say Paris was shelled this morning, but in the illusive palace one knows nothing of such things. . . . This city of spires and towers, of great hotels, museums and magnificent monuments, of boulevards, squares, wide streets, parks, huge buildings—a fairy place!

A good luncheon at Les Ambassadeurs; coffee and liqueurs amid the usual banter and blowing of straws, pidgin-English, and worse French. Then for a drive in the Bois, followed by Armenonville's. Well, it's a day for that. The Place de la Concorde, the Rue de Rivoli and Rue Royale, the Champs Elysées, are a furnace of heat and dust with the sun beating down on arid pavements, with the whirligig motor-cars and taxis twinkling like bright toys, and the workaday world of little people rushing about on its manifold business—no rest for them, poor devils! It is grateful to turn aside into the leafiest depths of the Bois and to draw up presently in that divinest of restaurant-gardens, the Pavillon d'Armenonville. Albeit it is deserted—except for two ultra-up-to-date Frenchwomen drinking coffee with a couple of bejewelled, expensive-looking young Jews. Here amid deep groves and shrubberies one listens to the hushed song of chaffinches and linnets, and through wreaths of cigarette smoke watches the flycatcher darting back and forth from his perch on the opposite railing. The Bois sleeps. Old men sleep on seats, head on breast, newspaper lying unheeded on the ground; nursery-maids sleep on the grass beside their perambulators and babies; middle-aged ladies, beggars, and slum-children sleep in cool places under trees. Even the waiters sleep, some of them, beneath the striped umbrellas which shade Armenonville's tables.

But in the Champs Elysées the current of life revives, and the finest "prospect" in the world is awhirl with motor-cars, taxis, and many other conveyances. The same, only more amazing, frocks are to be seen. (The leading note of fashion must be given to the world even though the Bosche is only forty miles away!) Once more the mind refuses to attribute this mid-afternoon scene to a city threatened with imminent destruction. For in the rippling surface of life one can detect no flaw. To reach the hard core of things one must go to the railway stations, to the churches, to the heart of the middle-class homes.

Yet towards evening a certain staleness, a certain dusty emptiness and dreariness seems to fall upon these streets. At tea-time Rumpelmayer's is stark empty. In the Rue Royale, the Faubourg Saint-Honoré, the Avenue de l'Opéra, a few *chic* little milliners, a few officials and business people are hurrying homeward. This is a pause between the heyday of afternoon and that other mysterious spell which transfigures the streets of Paris after dark. At Ciro's, in the warm gloom of a great white room whose electric lights are cunningly concealed, many officers and not a few beautiful ladies are trifling with champagne cocktails and coffee. Maurice, coal-black, grinning, paternal, with his native air of fatalism, proffers people coffee and cigarettes on an Oriental tray. It would seem, unchanging and still grinning, he will do that unto the end of time.

After dark the Boulevard Montmartre is peopled with ghosts. They walk singly and in couples, they walk noisily with men, they slide by in the shadows, peering up at you, they loiter under street lamps and stroll aimlessly in front of you, they sidle round the street corners and dart out of the dim recesses of shop doors. And if they see a man alone they creep up beside him, whisper to him, pluck him by the elbow, even call out to him at a distance of several yards. To one from the trenches it is a strange experience, this formless, nameless company of spirits—pursuing, importuning—here, there, and everywhere—so many and so hungry.

It would seem they steal out with the shadows, these ghosts, swarm out to meet the pleasure-seekers at the hour when the lamps are lit and the curtain of mystery descends upon Paris. Imagination calls a man to raise this curtain, to investigate this mystery. For while the dim streets are restless, and the taxis rattle by, and the tide of subterranean life runs strong, it is impossible to go to bed. . . . Get a breath of God's good air—clear away the cobwebs from the fevered brain! . . .

So the rickety *fiacre* rattles slowly down the Rue de Castiglione, under the great archway of the Tuileries, through a courtyard, across the Pont des Beaux-Arts which spans the Seine. Along the Boulevard Saint-Germain, past the listening statue of Voltaire. How silent and dark the river! How immense the overpowering mass of the Louvre on the farther side! Then into a labyrinth of old and narrow streets, tortuous lanes between high walls, vast buildings, courts and alleyways, many churches. It is impossible to recognise anything. . . . We are lost. No, the driver knows—that old man who must have driven a lifetime through these streets. Ah, we're in the Quartier Latin! And there is the Sorbonne, and there, after more tortuous windings, the dim rounded shape of the Panthéon seen dimly against a lightening sky.

The chimes of Notre Dame strike midnight.

Midnight, and the world asleep! A pale moon gazing down upon Paris—and loneliness and the screaming of cats. The pleasure-seekers have vanished back into the shadows, so have the puppets and ghosts. A nameless figure rustles by hugging the wall like one ashamed. A light burns in some student's window—some student poring over his books or keeping late company in his little attic. Otherwise the city sleeps, and sleeping, waits.

Ah! This Paris! It is like a woman in its mystery, its waywardness, and its passion; its pride and beauty and its joy of life; its comedies and tears, its magnificence and wickedness; its tremendous past and eternal future; its laughter at the destinies of men.

Five days since I left Abbeville station, and here I am (it is June 15th) at an Officers' Convalescent Camp, suffering from a new and up-to-date form of trench-fever. I came over a bit queer in Paris, went to the A.D.M.S., and he sent me straight off here to the coast, where I am likely to be for three or four weeks.

I am not feeling too well at the moment, but the thing will have to run its usual course, and in some ways it is a nice rest after the travelling and rushing about I have had.

The thing that worries me is that I fear I shall lose my very interesting and long-waited-for liaison job down South. There is a chance that they may keep it open, but I fear the M.O.'s here are apt to keep one some time.

July 2nd. After nearly three weeks in hospital, I am now practically all right, and have got a light-duty job in the A.P.M.'s office in Havre for a fortnight. I have only just started it, but it seems a jolly good job, and I like it much better than hospital.

Trench fever is unpleasant in the earlier stages, but these only last about a week. It is a sort of influenza and pulls one down a bit.

I have an excellent billet here, and comparative freedom, not much work, only a bit of letter-censoring and occasionally one has to walk out the "criminals" (*i.e.* chaps awaiting court-martial). The place is pleasant, and I find I know several people at the Base even now, so I shall not mind if I am here for some time.

As to the liaison job, I have heard nothing more of it, so it is not off yet anyway. Meanwhile, I am having lessons and also working at French by myself, and am improving by degrees.

The weather is lovely, sunny and hot, and a lot of people bathe. I read and write a good deal, but otherwise there is not much doing.

It is the first of August, and I seem to have been terribly slack with my entries lately, but the fact is I have been deeply immersed in work of another sort, and once I start in on anything I almost dare not put it down until it is finished.

I have changed my quarters, being passed fit, and am at the Guards Division Base Depot. I am to stay here until the authorities get a movement order from the Division, which makes me furious, as every day is precious. The red tape involved in these things is considerable. Meanwhile, of course, I do not know definitely whether the liaison job is still going.

There was an attempted air-raid last night, and everybody had to stand about in trenches for two and a half hours, but it came to nothing.

Havre is crowded with people and is not unamusing, but very expensive.

Leave looks absolutely hopeless; the latest G.R.O. is that one is not *eligible* before seven months since last leave, at which rate I would be lucky to get it at Christmas! However, one can only hope something may turn up, and when things look most impossible they sometimes come right.

August 24th! A bare three weeks since I was mooning around Havre, and now I am back again at the front. The Division is in action in the Third Army push. So far I am stout and well, and am acting Transport Officer. I take up ammunition and rations every night to the Battalion on the battlefield; not a pleasant job, but the shelling so far has not been bad. Casualties will, however, I fear, be heavy before the end, although the Second Brigade came off lightly. This morning at daybreak our Brigade went over the top, but our losses so far are uncertain. To-night, as I have to find them, I shall know.

Stephen Graham, the author, acts as my orderly. The whole countryside is alive with troops, and it reminds me greatly of September 1916, just after Jack's death, the battle of the Somme. Flies, heat, and dust are terrible, but they do not matter much as long as the Bosche is going the right way—and he seems to be.

I must get some sleep, having to ride all night.

The last three days have been trying, but I am at least safely through the present stage of the battle without too much misadventure. We have been lucky so far in the Battalion, losing only one officer killed and one hundred and thirty-five other ranks killed and wounded. The first day we advanced about a mile under heavy machine-gun fire. The second, we captured St. Leger. The Grenadiers caught it pretty heavy, most of King's Company being taken prisoner. While acting Transport Officer during the battle, I have been lucky on my twenty-mile ride each night, since for some reason or other the Bosche has not shelled the roads.

It is the first of September and I have emerged unscathed from the battle, though as an acting Transport Officer I was spared the worst of it. However, on reflection, I think I had quite an exciting enough time going up to the line and back every night. I would start off at about 6 p.m., ride all night, and get back just before daybreak. One night, owing to the Battalion advancing, I rode twenty-six miles.

The Battalion attacked twice, but came off pretty lightly in the show. The first Grenadiers caught it the worst in this Brigade. We were, however, up against the toughest place in the whole line.

I am still on the same job, but there is not much to do when the Battalion is out of the line. However, this will be a very brief spell. What is going to happen to me eventually, goodness knows. Stirling said something to me about going as A.D.C. "here," and that it had been proposed from "outside," but what he meant I don't know, but must try to find out, also who proposed it. Meanwhile I can do nothing but sit still and wait for something to turn up.

It looks as if everybody will be kept fighting for a long time to come, but of course things are going swimmingly. The Battalion killed a lot of Bosches, the order being "No Prisoners," so they did in everybody, including the blokes who put up their hands . . .

. . . Since writing the above I have had a riding accident and resume my scribbling in hospital. I was galloping along a track near Berles au Bois and went head over tip into a summer road. I got concussion and am battered a bit about the head and face. Indeed, I was knocked out for two hours.

Who knows, with the Bosche running, the war may be over before I'm sent back? They say I may be here anything from a few days to several weeks.

CHAPTER IX

PILGRIMAGE

The clash of arms had long since passed away when my sister Angela and I, one October day in 1919, stood on the highest part of the Somme battlefield—the Butte de Warlincourt—viewing that remarkable scene in the rich light of a calm Autumn morning. Already, it seemed, the aftermath had come—that aftermath which, following upon rage, despair, distress of spirit, brings to the sufferer a dreamless sleep. I had found my own anodyne during the first year of peace in beginning a novel when, after recuperating and being a Demobilisation Officer, I had left the Army.

And now before us the battlefield stretched afar like some wild, undulating moorland; it was only when we looked critically through spy-glasses that we perceived the whole area to be one of complete destruction; that it was too a vast cemetery. In general, the landscape was bounded by the wintry skeletons of trees, ghost-like, shell-wrecked, identifying such ominous spots as High Wood, Delville Wood, the Bazen, and Le Transloy. Only in the distance could be perceived a little hill. There was no sign of life, except where the ruler-straight line of the Bapaume–Albert road cutting across the foreground was dotted by an occasional lorry or whirling motor-car that suggested something of the strenuous paraphernalia of a warfare past.

After all, this Somme battlefield—it was the home of

the dead. And we soon started to pick our way along the sloping side of the little ravine which leads up to the one-time village of Flers, a certain light of anticipation in our faces. Nor could the way be easily pursued, for shell-holes of every size treacherously overgrown with weeds and vegetation, not to speak of wires, staves, and the naturally rough nature of the ground, everywhere beset our footsteps. It was impossible to go far without a fall. Hardly less common than shell-holes were the graves of the soldiers—a greying wooden cross leaning to an angle marked usually by the name on a metal label, sometimes by nothing at all, and sometimes by the inscription *To an Unknown Soldier* in indelible pencil. At each of these we paused. Wreckage of the fighting of 1916 not less than that of 1918 lay on every hand. Here it was a steel helmet, German or English, dented. comical-looking, once set upon a man's head, now a piece of empty steel; there a shred of uniform, musty-coloured, sodden, and often hardly recognisable, such a shred as one sees left by some tramp on a country wayside; again, it might be a completely rusted rifle or a gas-mask strangely discoloured and forbidding, Fragments of letters we found, photographs of women, and the stray names of men who had long since gone to dust. Year-old tragedies lurked on either hand: in this livid green, stagnant pool where a soldier's clothing and equipment, his respirator and rifle, lay adjacent to an oozing, battered grave; in that shell-hole where a blood-stained overcoat and steel helmet suggest what may have happened there.

The village of Flers signifies a handful of grey stones

on a bare hillside rising toward a little knoll where once a church may have stood. Heaps of salvage litter the way—heaps of iron wiring-stakes or pickets, piles of trench-mortar bombs and shells, piles of leather equipment, broken trucks from a light railway, many rifles, dug-out frames, and boxes of ammunition. Presumably there had been neither time nor labour to cart them away. As for the road Flers–Longueval, so clearly marked on the map—it merges hourly in the green-brown world around and is already grass-grown.

Thus we leave the living world behind. We, so laboriously picking our way along the grim and deserted valley, find ourselves without sign or sound of human life; mere specks upon the vast heath; alone with the larks, with the dead, with the silent portents of bygone strife. The larks sing from an atmosphere of calm unclouded blue; all is still and all coloured by the golden sunshine which seems to dwell not unkindly, not even sorrowfully upon the havoc, upon the tumultuous passions of mankind here laid to rest. Only the troughs of the valleys remain in shadow. No aeroplane drones overhead. No more from the eastward comes the fitful murmur of the guns.

We are glad for Jack's sake—and our own. Strange how the horror, the loneliness, the chill, the cruelty of earth can be transfused in beauty by the mellowing sunshine of an autumn day!

Dim shapes of terror threading a way through labyrinthine darkness are viewed by us as a reality for ever fled, so are the waiting hours of pain and of dread, the wanderings by night, the lurid dawns, the stricken, weary eves that must have haunted his last hours. So, full of recollections, we plod onward, glancing often at the map, which is an uncertain guide, and occasionally correcting our orientation by the still visible peak of the Butte de Warlincourt. For we know that our friend lies near.

Himself is merged in the deepening sunbeams of the early afternoon, in the dreaming peace of this nevertheless solemn scene. So typical a better Englishman, so handsome, and yet so strong a nature! Somewhere he lies near—on that hillside above the shell-stricken wood—this product of an Eton and an Oxford life; this sportsman and man of affairs; this solid and familiar figure on the crowded London stage. . . . What is the satisfaction of our search? What do we expect to find, and what to feel? It is as though some magnet, some occult, refined sense drew us on. This we could not explain. For, after all, the sunbeams are no more than mocking memories: the reality is underground—a skull, a few bones, a wisp or two of hair, a shred or two of khaki cloth. But to that we cling. We reach out to within a few feet of what once was. And with every cross we bend down to, puzzling out letters and numbers which time and weather have reduced to mere ciphers, a quick look of hope starts in the eyes. . . . It is not to be.

And as though to remind us of the futility of men's efforts to reach out for that which Eternity has already claimed—something rustles. We are come to a little wood consisting of almost symmetrical ashen-grey stumps, of many that have fallen, of shell-holes clustered so thick that not a square inch of undisturbed ground remains. A dusky figure now appears and watches us intently, grinning. It wears a kind of turban, a khaki jacket, white drawers, and puttees. Evidently an Indian left in this lonely spot to carry on the work of salvage, for now a small fire is perceived burning without a dug-out. Like the Spirit of Irony itself it mocks us; like some ghoulish denizen of another world it has stolen from its lair at sound of unexpected wanderers.

We continue our search unheeding, but with hope afresh. Heart, mind, the vital energy concentrate upon the search. The blue and gold afternoon waxes and wanes. Solitary, we climb up to a plateau the better to obtain a view, and gaze across to a handful of bricks in a hollow where Ginchy was, to the undulations beyond where Combles and Lesbœufs once existed. To the right lies the empty space of Longueval, with Delville Wood in gaunt nakedness above it, and, unobserved in a hollow, the railway station of Guillemont. All are one with the calm beauty of the October day. Around and in great multitude lie the men of the Manchester Regiment. Captain Stewart of the Black Watch and a brother officer have unfortunately fallen here. A little beyond are the troops of the Irish Division which notably captured Ginchy towards evening on September 14th, 1916. Between this point and the patch of tree-stumps that marks Lesbœufs, the Guards Division swept over the hill shortly after daybreak on September 15th of the same year. There lies in echelon the flower of the British Army, by its battered crosses, by its rotted bodies and free-given blood marking the milestones of the road they travelled three years ago. . . .

On an old battlefield many strange things are found. Orchard Trench remains much as it was when, in the grey of an early August morning, the 60th Rifles and Rifle Brigade attacked at great cost. Everywhere lies the ordinary *débris* of occupied trenches—bully-beef tins, biscuit tins, traces of half-executed work, and even traces of half-executed meals. An officer's—probably an artillery officer's—dugout remains even as it was left. What happened . . .? A dented enamelled white basin with traces of soapy water stands on a box; shaving tackle all spattered with soil and mud spreads itself upon an improvised table. Something of a meal remains—a marmalade jar with tin plates and rusted knife and fork. A pair of muddy, hardened, boots is set down near the entrance.

So engrossed are we seekers that we do not notice the rapidly westering rays of the afternoon sun or the oncoming of night. We do not even feel the approaching cold. . . . Will we find our friend, or do the dead lie too thick—are the crosses too many? We pause in our search, a profound disappointment upon our faces. Already sundown is here, and it is the hour of the frost. Already great shadows begin to lengthen across the battlefield, blotting out the hollow places, adding infinitely to the vast tragedy of this land.

What bitterness lies there! What bitterness in the heart that cannot break, in the scalding tears that cannot wash away what once was vital, in the mind whose wounds Eternity alone can heal!

With downcast eyes we turn our faces toward the west. The shadows gather. The frost comes down. A partridge calls. All that was mortal we leave. 'Twas not to be. We homeward turn. . . . Presently looking up, we perceive against the roseate sunset glow three high crosses set upon a little hill.

Shall we return? Shall we look upon the place
where sky and sand and sea unite?
Who knows? A voyage of discovery
ever ends so. Life is over-
crowded. Isn't it? . . .
We may never return.

EPILOGUE

(From *The Times*, January 6th, 1923)

"MEXICO OUTRAGE

(From our Correspondent)

Mexico City, Jan. 5th.

Mr. Wilfrid Ewart reached Mexico City on December 23rd from Sante Fé (New Mexico), with the object of finding new surroundings and quiet for writing his books, and took a room on the fourth floor, with a balcony overlooking the street, in the Hotel Isabel, in the quieter part of the town, away from the main business centre.

On the night of December 31st he returned to the hotel at 11.30. It is assumed that, attracted by the sound of firing in the street, where rowdy merry-makers were following the local custom and firing at random in the air, he leaned over the balcony and was shot. No suspicion was aroused in the hotel until the afternoon of New Year's day, when his body was discovered; but as it was a public holiday, the Consul and others were not informed until next day, when it was removed from the mortuary for burial in the British cemetery by Dean Peacock. Twenty-four representatives of the British colony, including the Club, Consulate, and Legation, attended the funeral."